21ST CENTURY GREAT GLOBAL DEPRESSION

The Perfect Economic Storm

Outskirts Press, Inc.
Denver, Colorado

OREST ANDREW HARRISON

Founder of
SurviveandThriveNow.com

The opinions expressed in this manuscript are solely the opinions of the author and do not represent the opinions or thoughts of the publisher. The author has represented and warranted full ownership and/or legal right to publish all the materials in this book.

21st Century Great Global Depression
The Perfect Economic Storm
All Rights Reserved.
Copyright © 2010 Orest Andrew Harrison
v4.0

Cover Photo © 2010 CIMSS. All rights reserved - used with permission.

This book may not be reproduced, transmitted, or stored in whole or in part by any means, including graphic, electronic, or mechanical without the express written consent of the publisher except in the case of brief quotations embodied in critical articles and reviews.

Outskirts Press, Inc.
http://www.outskirtspress.com

ISBN: 978-1-4327-5807-3

Outskirts Press and the "OP" logo are trademarks belonging to Outskirts Press, Inc.

PRINTED IN THE UNITED STATES OF AMERICA

A study in how we got here, what's in store ahead, and how we as a nation might emerge from the darkness.

Table of Contents

FOREWORD: SAVING THE AMERICAN EMPIRE x
DISCLAIMER xxix
GENERAL OUTLINE xxx

PRE-GAME SHOW
(singing of the national anthem)

1: **READY TO POP:** A NEARLY SIXTY-YEAR ERA OF CREDIT EXPANSION, MASSIVE ACCUMULATION OF DEBT, AND "LEVERAGING UP" AS TIED TO THE SPAWNING OF THE WORLD'S GREATEST CREDIT/DEBT BUBBLE OF ALL TIME 1

(batter walks out of the dugout)

2: **THE ENEMY WITHIN:** A GOVERNMENT LOSES ITS WAY, LACKS A RESPONSIBLE AND COHESIVE VISION FOR THE FUTURE 8

(batter on deck)

3: **AMERICAN CAPITALISM GONE WILD:** GREED, RECKLESSNESS, AND CORRUPTION PERMEATE WALL STREET 17

(batter walking to home plate)

4: **THE PERFECT STORM:** MAJOR ECONOMIC, POLITICAL, AND SOCIETAL HEADWINDS, AND THREATS TO AMERICA'S CONTINUED DOMINANCE IN THE WORLD, PLUS PRINCIPAL FACTORS LEADING TO THE PRECIPITOUS DECLINE OF THE AMERICAN EMPIRE 23

(batter steps into the batter's box)

5: **AMERICAN EMPIRE IN TROUBLE:** EERIE SIMILARITIES

TO THE COLLAPSE OF THE SOVIET UNION 29

(batter checks signals)
6: **OUR "UPSIDE DOWN" WORLD:** A GLOBAL COMMUNITY OF NATIONS FLAT BROKE PLUS DIRE CONSEQUENCES OF ENTITLEMENT PROGRAMS GOING BUST 33

(batter gets set)
7: **BITING OFF MORE THAN IT CAN CHEW:** GOVERNMENT AGENCIES AND PROGRAMS ALREADY RUN INTO THE GROUND ATOP NEW PRECIPITOUSLY GROWING OBLIGATIONS 38

(here comes the pitch)
8: **THREAT TO CIVILIZATION:** DERIVATIVES, THE MOTHER OF ALL TICKING TIME BOMBS; OUR 680 TRILLION DOLLAR GLOBAL CONUNDRUM 41

(swing and a miss)
9: **SOLUTIONS ELUDE US:** MODERN AMERICAN SOCIETY RELEGATED TO PETTY PARTISAN BICKERING AND PLAYING THE BLAME GAME 44

IT'S GAMETIME!
(and we're playing with a bunch of amateurs)
10: **CRACKS BEGIN TO APPEAR IN OUR BUBBLE-ECONOMY FOUNDATION:** RATE OF IMPLOSION PICKS UP STEAM AS EACH STRUCTURAL WALL GIVES WAY; THE EMPEROR HAS NO CLOTHES! 47

(batter dazed after being hit by wild pitch)
11: **THINKING THE PARTY WOULD NEVER END:** GETTING CAUGHT IN THE VORTEX OF CREDIT EXPANSION -- AMERICANS AND THE WORLD ARE CAUGHT FLAT-FOOTED 51

(rout of the home team begins)
12: **FAST TRACK TO POVERTY:** INESCAPABLE CONSEQUENCES OF A DEFLATIONARY DEATH SPIRAL -- ALL ASSET CLASSES ARE PULVERIZED!............................56

(three up, three down as visiting pitcher hits his stride and strikes out the side)
13: **REAL ESTATE -- AND WHY IT <u>MUST</u> CONTINUE TO FALL:** TRADITIONAL RESIDENTIAL REAL ESTATE vs. FORECLOSURES; A TALE OF TWO MARKETS 60

(home team outfielders collide chasing a routine fly ball; ball drops, three runs scored)
14: **DARK CLOUDS ON THE HORIZON:** EQUITIES MARKETS AND WHY THEY <u>WILL</u> <u>ULTIMATELY</u> CONTINUE TO CORRECT 65

(broadcaster announces major ticket price increases with the start of the new season)
15: **DEBT-RIDDEN CITIZENS ON THE BRINK:** HIGHER TAX RATES ARE ON THE WAY AND HERE TO STAY, PLUS OTHER UNINTENDED CONSEQUENCES OF MASSIVE GOVERNMENT SPENDING 73

(falling way behind...)
16: **IT'S STILL NOT TOO LATE TO THINK AND ACT AS A CONTRARIAN:** (BESIDES...YOU'RE IN GOOD COMPANY; CHRIST WAS ONE TOO)..80

(late innings...pulling out all the stops, calling in the pinch hitters)
17: **UNCHARTED WATERS:** BAILOUT NATION AND RELENTLESS MONEY PRINTING BY THE US TREASURY..86

(future hall of fame prospect expected to announce his
retirement upon unsuccessful bid at pennant)
18: **ENTER THE 20,000 POUND GORILLA:** NEGATIVE ECONOMIC IMPACT FROM AN AGING BABY BOOM GENERATION 90

(key players are suspended indefinitely
due to suspected steroid use)
19: **WOE TO GENERATION "Y":** PRAY FOR OUR <u>LOST</u> GENERATION 93

(visiting team announces plans to build new stadium)
20: **BOND MARKET BLOW-UP:** CHINA, JAPAN, INDIA, BRAZIL, ET AL. (CREDITOR NATIONS OF THE WORLD) HOLD THE KEYS TO AMERICA'S FUTURE, PLUS INTEREST RATES AND WHY THEY <u>MUST</u> CONTINUE TO CLIMB 97

(after a brief rain delay, our clocks get cleaned...)
21: **GLOBAL DEFLATION AND DELEVERAGING PLAY OUT:** "BEARS" ROAM THE EARTH UNOPPOSED! 102

(bottom of the 9th, it's a blowout!)
22: **ENTER, HYPERINFLATIONARY TSUNAMI:** LIVING IN THE TWILIGHT YEARS OF THE US DOLLAR: THE GREATEST TRANSFER OF WEALTH IN HUMAN HISTORY COMMENCES 105

(yer out!!! Signals get crossed as runner is thrown out
at home plate registering the final out)
23: **BEST CASE SCENARIO:** PREPARE YE FOR A PROTRACTED PERIOD OF STAGFLATION 110

(the crowd streams out of the stadium as the approaching storm spawns tornados)
24: **ANALOGY TO ARMAGEDDON:** 2/3 OR MORE OF WORLD COMMERCE IS WIPED OUT! GLOBAL UNEMPLOYMENT REACHES BIBLICAL PROPORTIONS AS 1/3 OF ALL JOBS PERISH FROM THE EARTH... 112

POST GAME WRAP-UP
("BRIC" nations [Brazil, Russia, India, China] win their respective divisions and are headed to the playoffs…)
25: **VROOM, VROOM…REVVING UP THE NEW ENGINE OF WORLD GROWTH:** "BRIC" NATIONS (BRAZIL, RUSSIA, INDIA, AND CHINA) AS WELL AS OTHER DEVELOPING NATIONS EMERGE AS THE SUPERCHARGER OF WORLD GROWTH 117

(falling into the cellar)
26: **THE RED DRAGON SLAYS THE ONCE ALL-MIGHTY EAGLE:** CHANGING OF THE GUARD; WORLD ORDER GETS FLIPPED ON ITS HEAD AS AN "AGE OF DARKNESS" DESCENDS UPON THE EARTH 120

(urgent need to rebuild our bullpen)
27: **OUR ENEMIES SMELL BLOOD:** AMERICA EITHER SHIFTS TO RENEWABLES OR SINKS INTO OBLIVION; AMERICAN ENERGY INDEPENDENCE IS AN ABSOLUTE MATTER OF NATIONAL SECURITY 123

(calling up our minor league lead prospects)
28: **REBUILDING AMERICA'S MANUFACTURING BASE:** AMERICA'S FUTURE HAS THE FOLLOWING SLOGAN/ LABEL WRITTEN ON IT: "MADE IN AMERICA"................ 127

(rebuilding the franchise)
29: DARE TO DREAM; REACHING FOR THE PINNACLE YET AGAIN ONE SMALL STEP AT A TIME: AMERICA'S RETURN FROM THE ASHES BEGINS WITH THE BELIEF THAT BETTER DAYS LIE AHEAD. (AT SOME POINT THE ONLY DIRECTION LEFT TO GO IS UP. 130

MY FAVORITE QUOTES AND EXPRESSIONS 135

FOREWORD: SAVING THE AMERICAN EMPIRE
(my personal rant)

I love my country…above all, I consider myself a <u>patriot</u>. A son of immigrants, ever since I can remember, I've been instilled with a profound sense of gratitude, honor, dedication, and devotion to the land of the free and the home of the brave, as well as a profound sense of respect for and admiration of America. At times, a less than perfect union, it can be said of our government that it has on occasion lost its way -- in the process becoming too overbearing, obtrusive, arrogant, ineffective, intolerant, uncompromising, irrational, and out of touch. Building our democracy has, after all, been a centuries-old experiment fraught with peril, and arrived at through trial and error.

Nonetheless, I am one who subscribes to the belief that America has (by and large) stood for principles of good and decency in the world. Historically, when we have made mistakes (there are more than a few examples) we have collectively striven to better ourselves and our less than perfect union, even though progress has often been slow. In just the past thirty-plus years, we as a nation have made tangible progress: I have personally witnessed an historic transformation in America as we've made strides to narrow the racial divide and close the gender gap. We won the Cold War, and in terms of technological advancement we've generated nothing less than a "moon shot" of historic progress. We've watched virtually every market including two of our largest (equities and real estate) soar to unbelievable heights, and we've grown vastly wealthier by every conceivable measure. We have also managed to remain the envy of the world -- at least until recently.

However (speaking strictly in economic and political terms), it appears that much of our wealth creation has come at a <u>very high</u>

FOREWORD: SAVING THE AMERICAN EMPIRE

<u>cost</u>. We have over the years thinned the pillars of our economy, abandoning fundamental economic truths in the process. Our stewardship has included progressively hollowing out our manufacturing base (once the envy of all the world) and substituting it with an unsustainable consumption-based economy. Having lost any semblance of cohesive and responsible fiscal policy, it appears we have taken to abandoning the notion of ever again balancing our federal budget. We (government and private citizens alike) have borrowed beyond any measure of sensible, responsible behavior to sustain our personal lifestyles and our empire. All good things must come to an end, however.

With the seizing up of credit markets in 2007-2008 and the simultaneous bursting of historic credit and debt bubbles, a seismic shift occurred in the behavior of the American consumer that will affect the way we live for generations to come. As **<u>borrowing on demand</u>** instantly became dead on arrival, a cash-strapped consumer was no longer willing or able to (as in previous recessions) do the heavy lifting in expeditiously springing our ailing economy back into recovery. As such, a global economic crash has begun which I fear has **many unwritten chapters yet to come.** Today, we find ourselves in an age defined by a <u>crisis of confidence</u> – as in the '70s, much of it emanates from the fact that Americans (as well as the global community) now recognize America's future to be not nearly as bright as previously perceived; unlike the '70s, today there is a growing global perception and recognition that our policies (past and present) are leading to an <u>abject mortgaging of America's future</u>.

This time around, the public perception and public concern involves (using Humpty-Dumpty as a metaphor for our economy) our not being able to put all the pieces back together again. Our current economic strategy takes no aim at fundamentally rebuilding, remaking, repairing, rebalancing, or redefining our economy from the ground up; instead it attempts (through massive increases in government spending and ever higher debt loads) to **temporarily** breathe new life into our ailing economy in an <u>all-out effort to sustain and preserve *current* prosperity</u>. This course of action is shortsighted as well as unequivocally desperate, and in the end will serve only to further bankrupt our nation. While no one denies the importance of addressing the concerns of America's citizens today, of greater importance is this: what will become of tomorrow? Of ultimate importance: <u>what will become of our children and their future?</u>

At the center of our current economic quagmire lies Americans' addiction to inexpensive goods (and oil, for that matter). Our meteoric rise in personal wealth is in part a direct byproduct of our addiction to a relentless stream of cheap imports -- products typically manufactured in third world nations by low cost labor. While on one hand, this arguably gluttonous behavior has caused Americans to amass possessions like never before, it has also -- as a consequence of trade imbalances -- helped inspire <u>federal budget deficits as far as the eye can see</u>. It has also contributed to the diminishment and decimation of our productive capacity as a nation, as American corporations have increasingly sought out low cost labor overseas to forge ever-higher profit margins here at home. (As previously mentioned, our <u>manufacturing base is hurtling towards obscurity</u>.) Our national mantra to grow our personal wealth **at any cost** -- no matter the ramifications -- has cumulatively led us down a path of egocentrism, at times dismissing our heritage and core historic traditions, which include abandoning a quest for instant gratification by focusing on the greater good, displaying a sense of national unity and call to service, self-sacrifice, sane fiscal stewardship of our economy as well as our personal affairs, saving up for a rainy day, etc. By all measures -- we, as a nation have **completely abandoned** the cherished notion of <u>living within our means</u>.

FOREWORD: SAVING THE AMERICAN EMPIRE

THE COSTS OF OUR FISCAL MISMANAGEMENT ARE TOO HIGH

As a consequence, we are relinquishing our sovereignty piece by piece as our federal debt and budget deficits grow, seemingly exponentially, far beyond our capacity to contain and/or reconcile them. Some in the world have begun to question America's sincerity and ability in ever fully repaying borrowed capital. Doing the devil's bidding all along…foreign purchases of US debt -- (although having slowed of late) -- the accumulation of US treasuries (US debt) by foreign governments ("creditor nations") as well as private and corporate foreign investors has helped keep our economy afloat. Keep in mind, this policy of ever-increasing ownership of ever-larger and more significant stakes in America has continued for some time.

Where this has gotten us: To paraphrase former presidential candidate Ron Paul regarding our burgeoning debt load: If the federal government were to sell every hectare of land that the government owns today (if, in other words, Uncle Sam were to liquidate his entire stockpile of real property/tangible assets), it would still not suffice to pay off our overall debt load. Our total federal indebtedness is by far the largest of any government in the history of man (as of this printing, more than 13 trillion dollars and rising rapidly; no less than 82 trillion dollars if you add government I.O.U.s to Social Security, Medicare, etc.), and is currently growing at breakneck speed thanks to a parade of bailouts and stimulus packages!

Our military budget in just the past four years (information obtained from an article by Jack Quinn) has increased over 26%; this as we continue to run historic multi-trillion-dollar annual budget deficits. We have spent over a trillion dollars on defense alone since the end of the Cold War as our military budget continues to rocket upward -- SOME PEACE DIVIDEND! Even as a self-prescribed military hawk I recognize the importance of observing the sober economic facts on the ground -- that budgets are neither absolute nor without limitations.

Other problems plague our union: In terms of the social fabric of our society today, we appear by most measures to be **losing** the battle against crime in America's cities as gun use, gangs, and drug use continue to escalate. Parts of many of our major cities are untenable; the vast majority of our borders, unsecure. In addition, our lack of motivation in taking the necessary steps to reform our oil-based economy into a more stable, independent (sovereign) economy based on renewable and/or indigenous resources leaves us more vulnerable than ever to even a small flare-up of inflation, let alone the emergence of hyperinflation. Our Federal Reserve policies aim to devalue our currency to a fraction of its former value as ever-growing calls emerge from America's major trading partners such as China, Russia, Brazil, and the Middle East, promoting the replacement of the US dollar as world currency. In sum, America as superpower has for quite some time been mismanaged to the core. Without an immediate and honest debate about the state of our economic affairs, a reality check, and a candid assessment of what we as a nation can and cannot afford, and where our priorities lie, the American empire itself faces the danger of extinction.

REGARDING INTERNATIONAL PERCEPTION OF UNCLE SAM...

America of late, has not been kindly portrayed, and rightfully so. Many in the world continue to criticize America for her gross and thorough mismanagement and mishandling of capitalism and the global economy. Others portray the United States as a nation in deep economic and financial turmoil -- a country so desperate to keep her economy afloat at all costs that she is willing to impose any measure (even if it means replacing one unsustainable bubble after another) to hold on to the status quo.

Proof positive: Over the past decade or more, aside from having nothing more than a bubble economy to show for, we have in recent years literally gambled away our prize institutions, corporations, and banks…the pillar of American and global capitalism, creating (now discredited) financial products such as C.D.O.s (collateralized debt obligations), M.B.S.s (mortgage-backed securities), etc. in the process. Furthermore (apparently unsatiated in its determination to self-destruct), Wall Street in recent years helped foster <u>speculative derivatives trading</u>, a largely unregulated trading platform and the ultimate **"apocalyptic"** investment vehicle. (Warren Buffet refers to derivatives as "financial weapons of mass destruction.") Our ratings agencies…Standard & Poor's, Moody's, Fitch, etc. -- up to their necks in culpability for the dire circumstances we now find ourselves in -- helped predicate the peddling and selling of a host of Wall Street's ill-conceived financial products, bonds, and instruments only to witness the equity and valuations of the underlying securities collapse alongside the very same firms originating them. Prescribing bogus "AAA" credit ratings to super-leveraged, fundamentally high-risk, often "worthless" securities, bonds, and financial instruments prior to the crash is now not only seen by the world as a major catalyst of today's sorry state of global economic affairs, but is viewed by many as the epitome of corruption. Some perceive our rating agencies' actions as <u>intentionally malicious behavior</u> -- <u>a collusion with US banks and brokerages to perpetrate a fraud</u>.

As a result of the shenanigans, most of us on Main Street (including the taxpaying public) are forced to absorb the fallout from Wall Street's schemes and endure the world's ire against American crony-capitalism. In sum, America, as fantastically blessed as it has been -- far beyond our forefathers' abilities to ever imagine or comprehend -- has been dealt both a black eye and a body blow as she finds herself discredited as a responsible world power and economic leader, discredited as the ultimate purveyor and arbiter of capitalism, and is increasingly recognized as a country in deep economic turmoil. The unthinkable has happened: America, the indispensable beacon of hope throughout the world is increasingly perceived as a country on her financial ropes, on the precipice of <u>insolvency</u> and <u>total economic collapse</u>!

Love his politics or hate his politics, I present to you this <u>altered</u> version of President Ronald Reagan's sweeping, poetic, and inspirational speech about a "shining city on a hill," for it aptly serves as a metaphor for our current political and economic predicament: Today, the shining city has fallen into disrepute with many of its buildings along the main thoroughfares (and elsewhere) suffering broken windows as well as some peeling paint. The lawns have not been tended to in a while and are seriously overgrown; the homes' curb appeal is fading fast. Most recently, leaks have begun sprouting from various rooftops and some neighbors have called in to report the smell of gas. Nearly one-third of the residents are complaining that they are "underwater" or "upside down" on their homes (instances where mortgage values exceed the market values of homes) and many homeowners are beginning to fall behind on their monthly mortgage payments as well as on their local and state real estate tax commitments. Jobs are becoming more scarce with each passing day. Add to this a crumbling city infrastructure, ever-higher crime rates, a dangerous over-dependence on oil for home heating, fueling our cars, transporting goods, etc., decades-long moral decadence and decay -- and we now have <u>more than just a few problems</u>! Today, given our sad state of affairs, our shining city itself is **<u>rapidly turning to the color of coal</u>**.

IT'S TIME (AS A NATION) TO FACE THE MUSIC, AND FACE OUR GRIM FISCAL REALITY

The title of <u>superpower</u> is not something in and of itself bestowed on the country with the most nuclear weapons, or the country possessing the most land, nor the country with the most inhabitants, trees, nor the highest GDP (gross domestic product). It is a title delineated (not to be too coy) in a manner similar to celebrity power rankings -- on the basis of a number of factors and criteria, not the least of which is <u>prestige and influence in the world.</u> Although I personally would like nothing more than to see the American empire

FOREWORD: SAVING THE AMERICAN EMPIRE

endlessly thrive on and to continue our tradition as undisputed global superpower and economic powerhouse of the world, no nation is at liberty to wear these titles in name only -- a nation must continue to earn them day by day.

In so saying, America has maintained the title of **superpower** not just because she has been blessed to hold the world's strongest economy for nearly a century, but also because of the plethora of aforementioned "psychological" and less tangible factors. Unlike many other empires throughout history, America's empire was not derived from nor preserved by brute force or aggression (at least, I don't subscribe to this belief). Rather, America's legacy has been one of military restraint and respect for other nation states. As a byproduct of our historically discriminating use of our military as well as other factors -- our symbolism of freedom in the world (America as beacon of hope), it has enabled our nation to win the admiration of other nations.

Today, however, American prestige abroad has fallen into the crapper, as in recent years our policies have portrayed America and Americans as inflexible, ineffective, undiplomatic, overbearing, unrestrained, even omnipotent; America as a military power has simultaneously been viewed as overly militaristic and far too unilaterally-acting. (Though there are surely examples where America need act alone, by and large it has been America's current military posture that has generated mountains [high Alps] of ill-will throughout the world toward Uncle Sam and his policies.) Restoring and rebuilding the world's <u>trust</u> and <u>respect</u> in America as <u>the</u> top-tier **discriminating** military power in the world will require a great deal of goodwill, diplomacy, and striking the right balance in regard to America and her partners abroad. *(Recently, I dare say the pendulum has swung so far in the opposite direction in terms of American foreign policy that it has become similarly ineffective, espousing a doctrine of appeasement with regard to foreign threats.)*

Nonetheless, today we <u>are</u> a superpower because the corresponding facts on the ground support this assertion. The more critical question however, lies in determining the length of time that America will be able to **maintain** her current dominant military posture.

Although some will likely disagree, I am personally convinced that a collapse of America as superpower would present a most ominous development to current geo-politics, creating a power vacuum with eager imperially-ambitious nation states jockeying for position. (As such, a collapse of America as superpower is likely to lead to escalating dangers and a heightened threat to our national security.) Preserving our empire by hoping against all hope that China and other creditor nations will continue indefinitely to underwrite the moneys needed to maintain our global dominance by virtue of massive new purchases of US treasuries is at best absurd, and at worst, smells of hypocrisy. Relying on getting "a little help from our friends" (and enemies) is not a sustainable energy policy either -- assuming that unabated streams of cheap oil will continue to flow from Iran, Russia, Venezuela, OPEC, etc. is a fool's game. Beating our chests wildly while proclaiming, "Booyah, we are the world's sole superpower!" won't do the trick either.

That said, as our options for maintaining global dominance continue to dwindle with each passing day, many in the world are increasingly questioning whether America can afford to maintain all of her vast global financial, military, and political commitments of the day: providing principal financial backing for the UN (United Nations), the IMF (International Monetary Fund), NATO (North Atlantic Treaty Organization), etc. (The fact is we cannot fiscally afford to maintain them by a long shot.) In sum, virtually any objective assessment of our predicament tells us that it is just a *matter of time* until destiny forces our hand, coercing us to degrade to a less influential power/status.

To further illustrate this point, former global financial powerhouses and Wall Street darlings Bear Stearns and Lehman Brothers, as well as giant insurer AIG, were quite recently perceived as "omnipotent", possessing rich and virtually unblemished histories, monster prestige and power rankings (as related to global investment banking), simultaneously possessing both huge asset bases and seemingly unlimited material resources. Yet these corporations were forced into bankruptcy virtually overnight when the public's worst fears were realized -- a recognition that their businesses were built on quick sand and that the underlying corporations were technically <u>insolvent.</u> In a strikingly similar manner, insolvent governmental entities Fannie Mae and Freddie Mac suffered comparably humiliating fates, crashing and burning seemingly overnight.

My concern? A belief that the **apple has not fallen far from the tree.** By almost every measure, Uncle Sam's fiscal state of affairs denotes a level of disarray and insolvency far in excess of the now failed former giants of finance and insurance. In so saying, it is not disingenuous to begin candidly asking ourselves if America's #1 global ranking of superpower is genuine, or just a mirage.

We are fast approaching a crossroads. No matter how many ways one may try to sugarcoat it, bankrupt is bankrupt. Spending our way out of the crisis solves very little and serves only to exacerbate our problems. As Euro Pacific Capital's Peter Schiff has reiterated time and again, it is <u>indebtedness</u> and <u>overspending</u> that is at the *heart of the crisis.* California (in deep financial turmoil) recently put the hard questions to its voters in helping it decide where drastic budgetary cuts should be imposed. Popular or not, Uncle Sam needs to take a cue from the Golden State. Drastically reducing our federal fiscal overhead now, simultaneously ceding a commensurate degree of international power, privilege and/or influence, is a necessary evil which this situation calls for. <u>Now's the time</u> to throw in everything but the <u>kitchen sink</u> to right our fiscal ship **before it's too late.** As it stands now, our current policy of <u>going for broke</u> while leveraging up our balance sheet to the point of oblivion (burdening our children with generations of escalating debt) is only detracting from our chances of building a sustainable economy in the long run.

One caveat to my proposal:
If it should turn out that Uncle Sam has already breached the

point of no return and that his debts are in fact irreconcilable (a view that is of late gaining support), I would rather see Uncle Sam (using a bankruptcy metaphor) file for Chapter 13 reorganization sooner than later, rather than meander as a zombie nation with unattractive future prospects only to end up in a Chapter 7 liquidation sale at a later date. Show me an America that's capable of making the tough and painful decisions in transforming herself into a fiscally more responsible, wiser, more self-dependent, albeit smaller (yet still influential) power and I'll show you a happy man.

THE SOLUTION: A PLEA FOR UNITY AND SENSIBLE LEADERSHIP

Given my desire to see my country succeed, I state emphatically: It is imperative that we put partisan bickering aside and put **country before party**! It's time for Republicans and Democrats to drop their focus on "Gotcha politics!" and work together shoulder to shoulder to put our country on a sustainable path to economic growth and continued world leadership. Extreme partisans in either party ought to be **marginalized**, rather than given an elevated platform from which to incessantly berate the other party as well as obfuscate issues, as common sense politicians need to take charge. **Whether you prefer to call our economy a train wreck, a financial tsunami, or the proverbial Titanic moments after it smashed into an iceberg, we Americans (Republicans and Democrats alike) are all on the same financial highway to hell.** We are all losing our prosperity, our home equity, our retirement savings -- as well as our future prospects -- at an alarming rate. Finger-pointing and incriminating ourselves on the way down simply lacks integrity. Each party must be willing to concede mistakes made and take responsibility for problems it created. (I'm pretty sure each party is up to its eyeballs in culpability for the economic morass we've landed in.)

There will be plenty of time to analyze what went wrong in the greater scheme of things if we, America's citizens, can just make it

FOREWORD: SAVING THE AMERICAN EMPIRE

to the end of the month with a roof over our heads and food on the table, if the small business owner can maintain payroll for a while longer while continuing to meet his or her monthly commercial loan obligations…if our city, state, and federal governments can keep our streets safe, our social programs active, and our bond markets stable enough to stave off widespread defaults. **We (Republicans and Democrats) are <u>all</u> running out of time.**

BEGIN THE EXTENSIVE PROCESS OF DISSIPATING THE GLOBAL CRISIS OF CONFIDENCE

Usher in a legitimate <u>Era of Responsibility</u> and kick it off with a grand <u>mea culpa</u> to all the world for our <u>botched</u> and <u>gross mismanagement</u> of the world economy: (I know what you're thinking, my conservative friends…get over it!) The world is suffering **disproportionately** alongside us as a result of our irresponsible, even perverted economic policies and Wall Street's fraudulent financial products, as well as mismanagement of the global banking system, etc. Next, pledge to the world that we will go back to our historic roots of sane economic stewardship and expeditiously move to repair the broken global financial system, completely reform the banking sector, and in the process totally overhaul our phony ratings agencies (Moody's, Standard & Poor's etc.). Pledge that we will defend the US dollar as world reserve currency even in the face of mounting debt and take the painful steps to balance our budgets and cure our budget deficits (eliminating waste and getting rid of pork barrel spending would represent but two of the necessary reforms). Let large insolvent institutions fail -- the government cannot continuously print unlimited supplies of dollars without destroying our currency in the process. (Mind you, defending dollar strength tells the world that we are serious about paying our bills and establishes the notion that we will not default on our debt.) Pledge to the world that beginning **today**, we Americans will begin the arduous process of relearning to <u>live within our means,</u> and we will not allow our cumulative future (the world's and ours) to be mortgaged as a result of excessive money printing.

Additionally, take immediate and drastic steps to get our economy off oil dependence, utilizing whatever means necessary in the meantime to meet America's energy needs (drilling for oil, increasing our dependence on nuclear, coal, and natural gas energies, upgrading our existing electric grid, etc.). Declare a de facto <u>state of emergency</u> regarding our oil dependence and pledge to spare no resource while applying our full national treasure to "going green" (money permitting). Once the task of getting off oil dependence is complete, then shift our focus to our allies throughout the world in helping them get off oil dependency as well (a gesture greatly in our national interest).

Finally, begin to reduce our military commitments throughout the world -- not because we want to, but because we <u>absolutely must</u> -- fiscally we cannot afford to maintain our nearly 800 bases throughout the world. Thus can Americans as well as the world begin to view America with a newfound measure of respect, trust, admiration -- even <u>inspiration --</u> as it has historically. Having America lead a new, future, "green" world economy begins with recognizing our shortcomings as a nation and having the moral and political courage to face the fire and take responsibility for our <u>wrongdoings</u>!

LEVEL WITH THE AMERICAN PUBLIC: TRUTH (AND TRANSPARENCY) HURT
(Drawing a line in the sand; an urgent need to apply ourselves hook, line and sinker.)

We need good politicians of all stripes to articulate to the American public that **ours will be the greatest generation of Americans yet**, that we will find the moral fortitude to bite the proverbial bullet and take the seismic and painful steps to totally restructure and reform our broken economy. Level with the public, telling them that our goals will not be achieved overnight, that it will take a number of years and that it may even be necessary to dig in for the long haul. <u>Things will likely get worse before they get better</u>.

Show that we're taking these various dramatic and drastic steps not only to improve the health of our union, nor to simply bolster it, but to literally <u>save</u> and <u>preserve</u> our union. **Translation:** It will require sacrifice from all Americans, as a day of reckoning has arrived when we must now begin the process of unburying ourselves from our current federal debt burden -- the government owes more than $40,000 for every US citizen alive today (man, woman, and child). Show how our plan will entail dramatically cutting overall spending, imposing a moratorium on social programs, shrinking the size of our federal budget -- all the while taking steps to promote a more efficient economy, cutting our military budget…living as a nation on <u>rice and beans</u> in an all-out effort to get our fiscal house in order. <u>Give realistic expectations for success</u>. Explain that it may take well in excess of a decade of spending cuts and other major efforts at rebuilding America's productive capacity, and even longer to wean America off her dependence on foreign oil. Convince the public that righting our economic ship while fighting a global war on terrorism cannot be done indefinitely by means of exploding budget deficits, nor by fervent use of a printing press. State for the record and apply in practice that we will meet all of our financial obligations **head on,** no matter the personal sacrifice. <u>State unequivocally that</u> **<u>America pays back her debt</u>**!

Finally, define and contrast our choices as a nation moving forward: a) continue our reckless fiscal ways of the past and in the process risk total economic collapse, complete loss of prestige, and loss of national security or b) sacrifice today like we've never sacrificed before, face (and grapple with) head-on the multitude of financial problems and economic challenges facing our nation today, and thereby inspire a <u>brighter future for America</u>.

A NATIONAL CALL TO SERVICE AND SACRIFICE; EMBRACING THE TIME-HONORED CONCEPTS OF

"BUILDING FOR A BETTER TOMORROW," "SACRIFICING FOR THE FUTURE," AND "PAYING AS WE GO" AS AN ALTERNATIVE TO OUR CURRENT GOVERNMENTAL POLICY OF ENDLESS BAILOUTS

(The concept of "living within one's means" -- working side by side and shoulder to shoulder for the greater good -- is not only an American truth, it is our heritage.)

Personally, I strongly oppose our current governmental policies which aim to give temporary relief to our economy while saddling future generations of America with burgeoning debt. I argue that it's not only irresponsible, unethical, and in every way deplorable policy, but that it is abjectly un-American as well as unpatriotic. Since when did the concept of building for a better tomorrow, sacrificing for a better future and paying our way in this world/paying as we go become not PC?

Generations of "great" Americans before us have espoused a motto of steadfastness, responsibility, overcoming obstacles, and sacrifice -- no matter the personal consequences. (Our historic mindset is certainly not one of "bailout mentality.") *Who can ever forget our forefathers' national call to service, unity, and sacrifice during the American Revolution? Remember their intense devotion to their cause -- pledging their lives, their fortunes, and their sacred honor?*

Americans in periods of crisis have time and again risen to the challenge, espousing personal responsibility, service, and sacrifice. It has been **our** generation's addiction to accumulating products and spending on services -- every kind imaginable under the sun…consumerism, materialism, and uber-shopping -- that has us *dancing with the devil* today. America's future generations have no culpability in this. Straying from our historic, time-tested, and treasured traditions has brought us to the precipice of financial disaster as our current solutions serve only to compound the problem. All the while, a global community of nations grows restless as it begins to

FOREWORD: SAVING THE AMERICAN EMPIRE

sense the impending <u>end of the American Empire</u>. One question, if I may…has all of the <u>binge buying</u> and <u>quest for cheap products</u> sapped every last bit of our cumulative brains?

P.S. EACH OF US MUST BE WILLING TO DO OUR PART…

As a father of a five-year-old, the concept of providing for and protecting my child is not a novel thing. It is commonplace for parents to do whatever it takes to ensure that our child's/children's future is brighter than our own. In so saying, if I, or most any other parent knew definitively that shoveling sh-t for the rest of our natural lives would ensure a prosperous future for our children, I'm convinced most of us would jump at the opportunity to do so. Humankind, by and large, is <u>wired</u> instinctually, intellectually, emotionally, genetically (if you will) to preserve and protect our offspring (oftentimes by any means necessary). Our government's numerous intercessions at helping today's ailing economy through use of controversial measures such as <u>excessive money printing</u> (which carries with it the effect of stifling future growth) in many ways flies in the face of our natural instincts as parents to preserve and protect our offspring. **Sadly, this leaves us with a <u>disconnect</u> or perhaps even creates a collision course between some Americans and government.**

Put in another way, our government as big brother believes that jump-starting our economy, while running up enormous trillion dollar debts, is a <u>justifiable trade-off</u> to having the world descend into economic depression, turmoil, and chaos -- the perceived "lesser of two evils." Many citizens (including many of America's parents, I argue) recognize the tightrope that government is forced to walk but nevertheless believe that **the ends don't justify the means** -- saddling America's future generations with crippling debt is simply too high a cost. This schism is resulting in a rising tide of <u>fiscal conservatism</u> which not only continues to grow in our country, but is sweeping throughout Europe as well, and which threatens to put

xxv

a damper on future monetary stimulus. Americans are increasingly choosing a path of having **the buck stop with our generation** so as to allow future generations of Americans a chance at true prosperity and the American Dream.

OUR CURRENT COURSE WITH DESTINY… RECOGNIZING THE SERIOUS AND IMPENDING THREAT OF HYPERINFLATION

(External and internal threats to the survival of the American Empire have never been greater.)

The threat of hyperinflation of our currency (monetary hyperinflation) as well as hyperinflation in the cost of products and services (price hyperinflation) grows with each passing day even if our government will not say so publicly. We have never before in our history printed money like it's going out of style, nor have we projected trillion-dollar deficits as far as the eye can see. Whether it lurks just around the corner or some time down the road, the emergence of hyperinflation (a possible byproduct of current US Federal Reserve and Treasury policy) would immediately put our nation in great peril. (Events of this nature might transpire slowly, playing out over the course of many months or years, or a catastrophic event could cause a severe hyperinflationary spike in the US currency in a matter of days or even hours -- compliments of a global run on banks.) Either way, should this doomsday scenario come to pass it would result in an immediate loss of sovereignty for our nation. Just from a hyper-inflating currency alone, prices on all products including commodities, food staples, and oil would be thrust much higher; America would instantly fall on the mercy of oil-rich nations (many of whom are not our allies) to keep our oil-reliant economy afloat (Americans forced to "pony up" increasingly worthless US dollars to -- in a good number of instances, hostile regimes -- or face the abject annihilation of the US economy).

If this scenario were to come to pass, America would in a New

FOREWORD: SAVING THE AMERICAN EMPIRE

York minute be unable to lead as before, and Americans would find themselves far less in charge of their own destinies than perhaps ever before in our collective history. Keep in mind, by the time hyperinflation would presumably set in, deflation would have run its sinister course, wreaking havoc on most asset classes. The combination of a one-two deflationary/hyperinflationary punch represents the absolute worst-case scenario for the prospects for the American Empire and remains a most unfortunate but plausible outcome to current circumstances.

Finally, if this economic "Armageddon" scenario were to happen, it would surely deal a knockout blow to faltering US prestige around the world and the US economy, as well as to virtually all US asset classes (including savings accounts and other paper instruments) once thought of as "safe havens."

In sum, not only is America's endless parade of bailouts, massive money printing, and our Federal Reserve's policy to inflate our economy not preventing the failure of the American economy and capitalism in the long run, it is **ensuring** the failure of America's future! It can be said (if I may be so bold), that the creation of inflationary forces within our current geo-political framework smells of treason. It is patently not in our current national interest to do so.

WHAT'S RIGHT ABOUT AMERICA: WE STILL HAVE SOME VALUES LEFT WITH WHICH TO LEAD...ONE BRIGHT SPOT

Economic realities aside, contained within our borders is **the promise of America** and the world. **Case in point:** New York City. A beacon of tolerance and unity in the world, this great city, and my beloved birthplace, symbolizes in many ways the best of America. A city which honors, respects, celebrates and idealizes originality, idiosyncrasies, and differences in all peoples, New York City is at its core "anti-terrorist." "The City," despite all of its shortfalls -- constant low-grade chaos, high traffic, smog, crime, social ills, budget imbalances, burgeoning commercial real estate vacancies, etc. -- represents a most incredible, endearing, and enduring city, espousing tolerance for all -- no matter one's creed, color, nationality, sexual orientation, or gender.

I personally believe that New York City was targeted by terrorists on 9/11 not only because it embodied the <u>heart of American capitalism,</u> but also because stripped down to its core New York City exemplifies what terrorists fear most…*universal* tolerance, unity, solidarity, and integration across an entire spectrum of peoples -- from differing socio-economic backgrounds, differing cultures, differing religious ideologies…people from all walks of life. As such, it <u>poses the gravest of threats</u> to those desirous of subjugating the world to their fanatical principals.

If it were possible to build a template of New York City and simultaneously duplicate it throughout all corners of the globe, **terrorism itself would die a thousand deaths!** A polar opposite to regimes espousing a one religion rule, New York City -- and by association America -- are thus destined to remain at the forefront of the global war on terrorism.

DISCLAIMER:

I write this book all the while hoping, even praying, that my economic prognostications turn out <u>flat</u> <u>out</u> <u>wrong</u>. A father of two, I need to quell my anxiety about a long, drawn-out economic quagmire, believing instead that America's prospects are still fundamentally sound, and retain (even against all odds) a sliver of hope as to the ability of America and her allies to produce the necessary positive economic reforms that will lead to a new **economic age of renaissance**.

I'd prefer to see US equity markets soar an additional 5,000 points straight up, but I'd need to know that it was based on <u>solid economic fundamentals;</u> I'd prefer to go to sleep recognizing that our current market rally is **sustainable** long-term vs. believing the alternative -- that we all *powerless pawns/bystanders* witnessing yet another US Fed-and-Treasury-induced sad chapter of American market mania and bubbles.

Furthermore, this book has been written within the context and framework of current global economics and geo-politics, and does not account for extraordinary events such as terrorist acts, unforeseen breakout of war or disease, explosion of crime in America (or elsewhere), social and political unrest, or a disintegration of national or international social order, to name a few. Any of these unfortunate events, as well as many others like it, would serve to compound America's (and the world's) economic problems and adversely affect chances and a timetable for recovery.

Never letting go of hope for a proverbial wind at our backs, let me bid America (as well as other nations in the world) **Godspeed** for a quick economic recovery. Finally, may it come to pass that my opinions, viewpoints, analysis, and economic prognostications (given their dire nature) represent a <u>worst case scenario,</u> not America's <u>best prospects</u> for <u>recovery.</u>

Orest Andrew Harrison

GENERAL OUTLINE and POSSIBLE OUTCOME TO THE 21ST CENTURY GREAT GLOBAL DEPRESSION

(No financial advisor, trend forecaster or market prognosticator operates with a crystal ball; anyone telling you he or she is certain of future events is a patent fraud. The stages outlined here are based on the current schematic of geo-political and economic "realities on the ground," as well as historic and contemporary technical trends. They are presented as a plausible general outline to future events -- dates listed below will likely vary)

Stage 1: (July 2005-March 2009)
LANDSCAPE FOR THE GREAT GLOBAL DEPRESSION IS ESTABLISHED BY VIRTUE OF A TRIPLE EVENT: A COLLAPSE IN GLOBAL REAL ESTATE PRICES, COLLAPSE IN GLOBAL CREDIT MARKETS, AND A COLLAPSE OF GLOBAL EQUITY MARKETS LEAD TO A 40%-45% WIPEOUT OF GLOBAL WEALTH: A **65-80 TRILLION DOLLAR GLOBAL DEFLATION** causes a rolling "topping out" of virtually all globally traded equity markets, real estate, and a broad spectrum of industries. The US residential real estate market leads the way down. Worldwide equity markets crash with breathtaking speed as company earnings fall off a cliff. (Corporate earnings -- on a global basis -- lie in ruins as most companies are forced to downsize/many poorly capitalized companies immediately find themselves struggling to survive.) Pillars of capitalism and world finance fall; the underlying fundamentals of the global economy begin to steadily deteriorate. A credit market freeze descends upon the earth, extending to all corners of the globe, precipitating a crash in global consumerism, as well as a radical change in consumer attitude toward credit and consumer spending. The world grows rapidly poorer as public perception of US-sponsored capitalism as wealth creator goes under

GENERAL OUTLINE AND POSSIBLE OUTCOME

fire and is largely discredited. A global derivatives bubble begins to unwind -- slowly at first, and progressively picks up steam (bear market rallies aside) as global deleveraging becomes the name of the game.

Not all at once, not necessarily in tandem, individual markets, industries, and sectors **top out** each according to their own pace and time frame, beginning with the US homebuilding industry (July 2005). The breadth and scope of the implosion in the US real estate industry is remarkable, as many homebuilding stocks fall 70%-80% in just the first twelve months of the corrective process. Mortgage insurance companies go bust as mortgage lending melts away. The "sub-prime" mortgage market blows up as deflation spreads from US homebuilders to US and global residential housing markets led by such states as California, Arizona, Nevada, and Florida. As credit markets become dislocated and "freeze up," lending literally dries up overnight. The US banking sector hits a top in December 2006 and within 24 months lies in a heap of ash. The US equities market finds a top in October 2007 and plunges by nearly half in less than eighteen months. Even so-called recession-proof industries prove to be anything but…the strategy of investing in "coke, smokes, and drugs (pharmaceuticals)" pushes indexes higher, but for only a brief moment. The rate of acceleration in the contraction of the global economy gains strength. Initially, markets sell off according to the 1929-1932 US Great Depression Era playbook.

Stage 2: (MARCH 2009-mid 2018+)
<u>BULK</u> OF THE 21st CENTURY GREAT GLOBAL DEPRESSION'S <u>ACUTE DEFLATIONARY PHASE</u> PLAYS OUT WITH GLOBAL DELEVERAGING HITTING ITS STRIDE, SEVERELY DEPRECIATING GLOBAL EQUITY, REAL ESTATE <u>MARKETS, ETC.</u>: Bear market technical rallies and temporary pockets of economic strength aside, global economies begin to contract and implode at an alarming rate. Global unemployment begins a steady ascent and ultimately skyrockets with double digit

unemployment becoming the norm. Talk of a deep recession dissipates as use of the term "depression" increasingly becomes more common. The world grows impoverished, even destitute. Free market capitalism as we have known it is dead (R.I.P.), as more major economies of the world turn retrograde. The bankrupting of whole countries begins (Iceland in 2008, followed by "PIGS" nations -- Portugal, Italy/Ireland, Greece, Spain, etc.) with more countries to follow. Real estate markets continue to correct and nosedive as commercial real estate (one of the last markets to correct) continues an historic awe-inspiring plunge. Global equities markets implode as P/E multiples severely contract to reflect the widespread collapse in earnings. Tax rates trend higher across the board; interest rates begin to climb as ratings agencies' downgrades of sovereign debt commences. Markets complete <u>the vast bulk of their respective crash cycles</u> as global equity markets are wiped out to the tune of 75%-90% plus. Global real estate (mean) valuations decline by no less than 45%-60%. Worldwide deflation and deleveraging now account for a **WIPE-OUT OF BETWEEN 175-200 TRILLION DOLLARS OF GLOBAL WEALTH.**

Stage 3: (late 2018-2022)
<u>AFTER A MULTI-MONTH OR EVEN A MULTI-YEAR RESPITE</u> FROM MASSIVE DEFLATIONARY AND DELEVERAGING (SELLING) PRESSURES AND A PRECIPITOUS CONTRACTION OF THE GLOBAL ECONOMY, MAJOR (WESTERN) ECONOMIES (G7 AND THE LIKE) CONTINUE TO FURTHER DETERIORATE, AS THE <u>GLOBAL UNEMPLOYMENT PICTURE CONTINUES TO GROW MORE BLEAK: "U6" unemployment -- the broadest measure of unemployment -- spirals up from nearly 20% to reach Great Depression levels of 25% or more.</u> Global equity markets (specifically those in the West) <u>retrace</u>, <u>bounce along the bottom</u> -- staging rallies at times -- and slowly but surely <u>continue the process of retreating to new lows</u>. Exacerbating already dramatically weak economic conditions on

the ground, America's aging baby boom population begins to weigh heavily on its economy. Global bond market troubles and defaults cause universal spiking of interest rates, which leads to a battering of an already flatlining global economy. Tax revolts become commonplace. Coincidentally, faster-growing/developing "creditor nations'" economies begin to stabilize, recover, and increasingly take market share (global gross domestic product) from more established western nations as they become the new engine for world growth. **GLOBAL DEFLATION NOW ACCOUNTS FOR A WIPEOUT OF NEARLY ¼ QUADRILLION (US) DOLLARS.**

Stage 4: (2023-2032+)

THE WORLD, HAVING BEEN RAVAGED BY THE PERFECT ECONOMIC STORM, IS LEFT UNRECOGNIZABLE EVEN COMPARED TO JUST A FEW YEARS PREVIOUSLY: INFLATION AND/OR HYPERINFLATION TAKES ROOT; GLOBAL INFLATION RUNS RAMPANT AS OIL SHOCKS, PRICE SPIKES, FOOD SHORTAGES, PANIC, RUN ON BANKS, ETC. TYPIFY LIFE DURING THIS (FINAL) PHASE OF THE 21ST CENTURY GREAT GLOBAL DEPRESSION. Virtually the entire globe is affected by an historic plunge in the US dollar, including anyone exposed to US dollar-denominated investments or US bonds, as well as all holders of US dollars (current world reserve currency). A global bond market bubble continues to implode, leading to substantially higher interest rates in the US and abroad. **GLOBAL UNEMPLOYMENT REACHES UNPRECEDENTED, HISTORIC PROPORTIONS AS 2/3 OF WORLD COMMERCE MELTS AWAY.** The world grows increasingly desperate as extreme poverty, hunger, disease, and human suffering grow to an unimaginable scale: civil unrest, crime, social disorder, war, as well as conflict rule the day.

Emerging from the rubble, real estate as well as other tangible assets classes stage a comeback -- with a vengeance! Commodities markets **explode to the upside** as a result of an ever-weakening US dollar; gold, metals, "softs," grains, oil, etc. <u>soar to unprecedented heights!</u> (The caveat? They do so against a backdrop of a crashing US currency.)

When all is said and done almost no one is left unscathed. Left standing, surviving the monetary and economic onslaught are a <u>select few</u>...a group of the most nimble, contrarian, and/or forward-thinking investors and entrepreneurs -- those who saw the writing on the wall and took steps to de-lever, safeguard their portfolios against both deflationary as well as inflationary outcomes; those who traded both "long" and "short," spreading their assets in a variety of asset classes: real estate, commodities, precious metals, select equities, and currencies.

1

READY TO POP
A NEARLY SIXTY-YEAR ERA OF CREDIT EXPANSION, MASSIVE ACCUMULATION OF DEBT, AND "LEVERAGING UP" AS TIED TO THE SPAWNING OF THE WORLD'S GREATEST CREDIT/DEBT BUBBLE OF ALL TIME

When irrational lending standards led to credit on demand…what went terribly wrong

A principal function of banks and brokers alike is to pursue new credit card customers, mortgage holders, as well as car and other loan applicants; to do everything in their power to lure in new clients -- offering every incentive under the sun to get customers to borrow more. There's nothing wrong with doing so -- after all, business is business, and courting and soliciting new customers is routine (even essential) business practice. It is at the point when lending standards are completely thrown out the window, when routine business practice morphs into a **policy of playing with fire -- or more appropriately, a death wish.**

That said, banks were not the only ones up to their necks in culpability -- the consumer showing an unrestrained desire for credit helped fuel our recent spectacular era of credit expansion. Had we in our cumulative quest to borrow shown a dose or two of common sense, a degree of restraint, and most importantly mitigated our use of credit, we could potentially have ushered in yet a new leg up in the overall boom cycle; instead, we are left to administer over one of the greatest economic and market **busts** in mankind's history.

To be fair, most Americans including yours truly (I confess I enjoyed receiving unsolicited offers for credit from time to time, especially when the offer included no annual fee), benefited greatly as a result of easy credit as it provided us leverage to instantly *upgrade* our lives, homes, grow our businesses, extend our schooling, travel the world, etc. As with all things however, borrowing has its limitations; it was at the point that America and Americans -- all…private citizens, small businesses, not-for-profits, multi-national corporations, municipal and state governments, our federal government -- lost our collective minds, going into debt "up to our eyeballs" when the system, in effect, broke down. As we began feeling the generational effects of a reversion to the mean (spurred on by a vicious credit contraction) all hell appears to have broken loose.

Otherwise, our historic era of credit expansion (post-World War II until recently) has in many ways sustained the nation well, allowing businesses and consumers access to capital, vastly growing the nation's wealth in the process. *What then, specifically could cause us to fall so far off the track?*

Many of the seeds of today's problems were planted long ago, the chief culprits among them being excessive government deregulation of the financial industry, unscrupulous Federal Reserve rate policies, as well as outright corruption in our banking and financial system. Once lending standards had **deteriorated beyond the point of any rhyme, reason,** or **rationality** our epitaph was being written -- most of us just didn't know it at the time. Our real estate mania masquerading as "the" principal economic engine for our economy just a few years back, in addition to being totally unsustainable from the perspective of economic policy, spawned a maniacal amount of froth in our overall economy. By the time Capital One Bank launched its infamous advertising campaign "What's in your wallet?" the Rubicon had already been crossed and our global economy was doomed...at the precipice of a historic downturn. (Heaven forbid that Cap. One or other banking entities should lose sight of their *prime directive* of focusing on growing their customer bases and maximizing record profits for even a brief moment to look around and recognize that Rome was burning!)

As Capital One launched this aggressive advertising campaign slogan courting new customers (with a vengeance!), economic realities on the ground were painting a bleak picture of a global consumer thoroughly **saturated** in debt to the point of exhaustion. Just in America alone, the typical consumer (at the time) possessed an average of eight credit cards with median revolving balances of between $8,000-$9,000 (mostly high interest debt accruing daily), hordes of unpaid bills to boot, and picture licenses most closely resembling the very same zombies portrayed in the Capital One commercials (reflecting an appearance of the walking dead). Some credit card holders at the time carried (and carry to this day) credit card balances far exceeding the national average. All told, it was not long after this ad began to air that our economy (and by extension the world's) began its death march straight into the bowels of hell, contracting at breakneck speed. The arduous process of capital destruction had commenced, which would serve to eventually clean out the excesses in our financial and capital systems. **For every yin, there is a yang.**

Talk about predatory lending...

At the pinnacle of the mania as a ceaseless array of credit card offers were flying at Americans in all directions, other components to our superheated, credit-driven economy were playing out as well. Mortgages, car loans, personal loans -- you name it -- were offered to almost anyone, at any time -- **on demand**, often with very few questions asked. Banks practically stalked their prey and lifeblood, the American and global consumer, by offering credit to both young and old. At times it seemed all you needed was a heartbeat to get approved for credit -- occasionally you didn't even need that. During the boom years of the bubble you could get credit as a **top tier credit risk** with a credit score in the (pitiful) 300-400 range, or even if you had previously filed for bankruptcy, so long as you were willing to pay a few extra percent interest (premium) on your loan/credit card or agree to pay higher closing costs on your home loan. If you had assets or had no assets at all -- it didn't matter much -- you were a <u>lock-in</u> for credit. If you owned a home you could easily get a 1st mortgage or home equity loan; if you didn't have enough equity to cash out but still needed a loan, equity would oftentimes be "<u>provided</u>" to you -- at no additional cost, compliments of unethical real estate appraisers. (**How this worked:** To make sure you would qualify for a loan and meet required income-to-debt or asset-to-debt ratios, your mortgage broker [typically <u>hell-bent</u> on collecting a commission] would work tirelessly by networking with unscrupulous appraisers who would prescribe fictitiously high and/or unrealistic appraisal amounts to help bypass underwriting protocols.) If you rented an apartment or lived at home with your parents you were a shoo-in for credit. If you owned a pet hamster you could never be denied credit for any reason. Stalkers could get credit, the unemployed would get credit; if you were living under a bridge or were just flat-out down on your luck, you could get credit so long as you asked nicely. If all else failed and you still couldn't get credit, you might try faking your employment information on your application, embellishing the amount of reported income, or reporting bogus assets -- so long as you promised not to do so consistently (once or twice was okay). If you tried all of the above techniques and you still (for some bizarre reason) could not get credit, presenting a **phony alias** would likely do the trick. (I stipulate that this scenario might require some due diligence on your part in obtaining the appropriate numb nuts for the transaction.) *I ask therefore, is it any wonder that in such a free-wheeling environment so-called "<u>liar loans</u>"*

*(no income verification, no documentation, no proof of assets, no cash down, no closing costs -- **no nothin'**) were so popular at the time?*

Did I mention that it was not uncommon to find some cash-starved, super-leveraged souls applying for and qualifying for two, three, or even more loans on their primary homes, compliments of a combination of bank loans and/or **owner financing**? Did you know that in certain extreme instances involving criminality, some brokers even managed to pull "phantom" homes out of the ether to qualify clients for mortgages and/or other personal use "cash outs"? In the era of easy credit, documents were routinely falsified, in a multitude of instances fake collateral used. Scams of all stripes ruled the day in the go-go days of the real estate mania.

Finally, given the <u>level</u> of risky, unethical, irresponsible, and corrupt behavior, is it really so surprising that the unwinding in the markets is so great, why this time our recession doesn't feel like so many others before it, and why we have a <u>full-blown global economic crisis</u> and <u>global financial meltdown</u> on our hands?

Something for everyone...

How could we throw such a spectacular and reckless <u>credit expansion party</u> and not invite gullible investors and speculators into the fray to gamble away their hard-earned moneys by whetting their appetite for risk? These money-men and women were enticed by ever-rising higher risk/reward products, higher leveraged securities, derivatives, as well as exponentially growing access to <u>margin</u> -- "credit" extended by brokers to their clients to trade securities. (Mind you, the pre-eminent investor of our time, Warren Buffet, categorically <u>dismisses</u> trading on margin, in essence equating it to gambling.) As <u>access to credit</u> continued its forward march, <u>trading</u> of increasingly high-risk financial products such as **futures** and **options** became the norm, helping to satisfy even the most aggressive adrenaline junkies ("trading" as opposed to investing being the operative word). Eventually for the truly insatiable… <u>futures options trading</u> was born. <u>Trading futures options (especially while trading "on margin") denotes (for all intents and purposes) the riskiest "investment" scheme ever created by man, making casino and racetrack gambling appear **excessively tame**</u>. Once again at the epicenter of the gambling mania, excessive borrowing/lending/credit was <u>the</u> catalyst in allowing excesses to build up as everyday (PC) terms such as "<u>leveraging up,</u>" "<u>trading</u> stocks," and "options <u>investing</u>" were devised, masking the true nature of the 24-hour international **gambling** casino.

The immediate aftermath…

With the abrupt bursting of the credit bubble, a sense of horror began to spread to all corners of the globe, many realizing for the first time the true extent to which they were <u>overleveraged</u>. Many a good citizen in the world was thus caught inadvertently on the front lines of a giant bubble deflation with multitudes ultimately <u>self-destructing</u> in the process. Some, we later learned, ended up gambling away their homes, credit ratings, businesses, retirement accounts, etc. Others…many corporations, banks, (global behemoths included) municipalities, states, charities, etc. -- the list of those effected goes on and on -- bankrupted themselves (often overnight) as it became clear they'd staked their investments on mountains of risk. All told, healthy balance sheets were gambled away as investors' and stockholders' futures, personal assets, workers' livelihoods, etc. were forfeited for the lure of high profits.

The carnage was comprehensive: world governments, much a byproduct of their own deleterious policies, fared no better as weakening economies and crashing tax revenues kicked off a series of sinister ramifications with many nations suffering an evaporation of national wealth, uncertain and unpredictable futures, exploding debt loads as a consequence of excessive money printing to stimulate economic growth, massive budgetary imbalances, threat of impending declines to national security and sovereignty due to a specter of falling future revenues for defense spending, and a debasement of currencies. <u>The era of easy profits was over; a new era of intense losses and high volatility had arrived</u> -- **the mother of all crashes** had begun in earnest.

2

THE ENEMY WITHIN
A GOVERNMENT LOSES ITS WAY; LACKS A RESPONSIBLE AND COHESIVE VISION FOR THE FUTURE

Shortcomings of Federal Reserve policy... governmental overspending, overreaching

Over the past few decades, politicians in Washington on both sides of the aisle helped predicate and promote the building up of America's house of cards <u>economy,</u> leaving it in a state of shambles totally <u>unready</u> and <u>unprepared</u> to engage an **economic earthquake** of 9.0 magnitude on the Richter scale. (The earthquake mind you, is a direct consequence of botched economic policy as well.) The stewardship of our economy has been so pitiful, in fact, and the steering of our economic helm so negligent, that it makes the political fallout from Katrina by comparison appear small. America's politicians slept at the wheel whilst our best opportunities came and went to repair America's burgeoning budgetary problems as well as to help prepare for a rainy day.

We had numerous chances to begin weaning our economy off oil dependence and onto alternative indigenous energy sources and "renewables" ("green" technology). Once the Cold War had ended we had an unparalleled chance to use the so-called "peace dividend" to balance our federal budget; instead (except for a brief stint in the late '90s), we allowed our federal budget to ceaselessly grow, exploding to ever new heights. (Currently the US federal government owes creditors from around the globe more than $125,000 per family of three!) During the height of the baby boom's productive working years, we had a chance to…no, we had an absolute <u>imperative/ mandate</u> (as a nation) to reconcile our books. Instead of preserving capital, building surpluses to fund future Medicare, Medicaid, and Social Security benefits (as well as federal, state, and local government pensions) we pissed away our most critical years, drawing against funds year in and year out rather than placing them in a lockbox. (A veritable and massive <u>nest egg</u> is needed from which to fund a growing class of retirees as exemplified by the aging baby boom generation.) Every major opportunity to lead government in a fiscally responsible manner with a slant toward the future Washington flat out blew, spending our valuable tax dollars like drunken sailors.

Although Uncle Sam has (admittedly) kept Americans safe from new major acts of terrorism since 9/11, at stake is our ability to thwart future security threats -- hard to do when multi-trillion-dollar deficits year in and year out are bankrupting the nation. Cumulatively, shortsightedness by politicians in Washington not only reflect an "oops" moment -- it is likely to directly lead to pain and suffering on an <u>unimaginable scale</u>. Surely, there must have been some leaders with the mettle to present a more inspirational vision for America than to foster a national consciousness of consumption to the point of <u>insolvency</u>. Now we have reached a point at which without <u>radical budgetary reforms</u> **the American Empire may be <u>lost</u>.**

Could you imagine the ramifications if you or I managed a company we were entrusted to run by fiscally burying it into the ground, operating it <u>unprofitably</u> year in year out for decades on end with current earnings projections showing heavy losses now and for the foreseeable future (at least the next <u>decade</u> or more)? How much time do you think we would be granted before shareholders would be "off with our heads"?

21ST CENTURY GREAT GLOBAL DEPRESSION

Our current economic recovery playbook...LOL (laughing out loud):

The United States government pours out a <u>virtually endless supply of money</u> in an effort to stabilize the global economy and unfreeze the credit markets. Aside from engendering a strong rally in the equity markets, the <u>underlying fundamentals of the economy continue to weaken</u>: real estate continues its retrograde march, with unemployment spiraling upwards to double digits; global trade and consumer confidence levels remain flat and/or are falling; global economies (barring a temporary stimulus-inspired blip into expansion/positive territory) demonstrate a downward path of least resistance -- only recently contracting at the fastest pace since the Great Depression; federal, state and local revenues continue to (by every measure) crash; company earnings, having already fallen off a cliff continue to bounce along the bottom of a ravine; the global banking system remains largely inoperable, still loaded with toxic debt (in spite of credit spreads having eased); credit markets remain largely frozen as availability to credit continues to contract; national debt loads -- especially those of G7 nations -- continue to skyrocket to stratospheric levels; major industries in our economy (especially banking, finance, mortgage, homebuilding, auto manufacturing, etc.) continue to flirt with insolvency, are on respirators, or barely turning a profit, having sustained tremendous damage in recent years. Other industries -- retailing, shipping and commercial real estate -- are on or headed to their financial ropes.

Adding to the uncertainty, no one knows precisely what ramifications lie ahead as a consequence of our current economic policies, as our government has made unprecedented moves to nationalize (socialize) broken industries: banks, auto, mortgage, insurance ... and eventually the homebuilding industry, perhaps? Concerns continue to mount as to whether we will soon be facing a full-blown currency crisis from our historic and unabated printing of US dollars, yet at the same time it does not appear that we are thus far getting a good "dividend" on dollars spent. (Governmental inefficiency, waste, and in some instances poor allocation of moneys have plagued government's recent bailouts and spending sprees.)

A growing divergence? Although we have witnessed an about-face, a positive shift in the fiscal behavior of both US consumers and corporations in terms of <u>deleveraging</u> and <u>reducing risk</u>, <u>our government has thus far not batted an eye</u> to try to reverse the behavior (excessive spending) that has helped bring on so many of today's problems in the first place. While consumers have begun reining in their purse strings, reducing spending, and focusing on debt reduction and savings -- *and* corporations have begun downsizing, choosing to focus on debt elimination, higher capitalization rates, and shoring up of balance sheets, the vast majority of world governments (led by the US and the West) continue their old ways of doing business -- in fact demonstrably accelerating the pace of budget deficit growth, expansion of financial commitments and "leveraging up." *[To be fair, present data has begun to portray a releveraging by the US consumer.]* No matter, a growing mood of discontent and disenfranchisement among many of the world's citizens now threatens to *derail and/or scrap our current economic recovery playbook* as they increasingly demand accountability for (tax) dollars spent.

Calling a spade...

Listed below are some of the more prominent chief architects of the 21st Century G.G.D. (Great Global Depression): The list includes notorious politicians, influential business leaders, as well as key members of the nation's "brain trust" -- all with access to the bully pulpit. As history is likely to reflect, these men (in positions of great power) often proceeded and acted with either total naïveté, blind optimism, greed, or just plain cluelessness as to the meaning of proper economic stewardship. Whether or not they acted maliciously or whether they deserve the benefit of the doubt…they helped put our economy -- and by extension the global economy -- in great peril. Drum roll please…

President George W. Bush touted the ill-fated statistic regarding record high (historic) US homeownership rates as a <u>key accomplishment</u> of his administration. This **"success story,"** as it turns out was built on a foundation of shaky sub-prime mortgages, risky adjustable rate loans, other bogus loans sporting so-called "teaser" rates (mortgages initially set with low enough rates to allow prospective buyers to complete their purchases only to -- as is often the case -- default a few years later), reverse mortgages, no document/no income verification "liar" loans, etc. In addition, this economic "achievement" was often peddled by a slew of sleazy, unethical mortgage brokers and brokerages, high-stakes gamblers masquerading as banking institutions, and unscrupulous real estate appraisers. Espousing a philosophy of lower regulation, especially in regard to financial markets, George W. Bush oversaw and inspired a period of recklessness on Wall Street which included the peddling of C.D.O.s (collateralized debt obligations) and other "bad paper." In hindsight, we now know all too well that these notes/loans were so volatile and dangerous that they should have been sold containing warning labels "<u>armed and ready to self-destruct in the near future!</u>"

When all is said and done, and in no uncertain terms, history will record that our government's unofficial policy of "putting <u>every single American</u> in the homeownership class" **created** an historic real estate bubble, which directly led to a sub-prime mortgage meltdown, and ultimately kicked off the 21st Century Great Global Depression. (As I describe in detail later in this book, a series of cascading problems led the economy down, beginning with the sub-prime housing meltdown, an ensuing residential housing crash, a worldwide banking freeze, a collapse in consumer spending, an historic collapse in company earnings, and a crash in global stock markets.) Talk about <u>unintended consequences</u>…**kudos Mr. President, for a job well done!**

THE ENEMY WITHIN ➤

Federal Reserve Chairman Alan Greenspan, architect and author of the **Era/Age of Bubbles,** was directly responsible for policies which led to a **superheating** of the US economy and subsequent crash by his unwillingness to allow for the natural cycle of (periodic) recessions to cleanse imbalances in the free markets. Instead he helped engineer one bubble after another. Many economists today credit Mr. Greenspan's irresponsible management of interest rate policy -- specifically his brainchild (following 9/11) to reduce the federal funds rate down to 1% and to hold it there for far too long as the gas which fueled the historic real estate bubble. At the height of the boom, our real-estate-inspired economy was superheating right before our eyes (plain for all to see) with grandmothers literally coming out of retirement to flip homes. Where was the Fed in taking the obligatory steps to cool our economy? Shouldn't this have been an appropriate time to caution citizens and sound the alarm for "irrational exuberance" (an infamous slogan uttered by Greenspan earlier in his career in the late 1990s)? Aside from warnings from a few stray journalists and market watchers, the Fed remained steadfastly silent. Any seasoned banker worth his or her salt knew that our policies of **credit on demand** were perilous and would likely end in total **financial annihilation and disaster**…that 20%+ year over year increases in real estate valuations was unsustainable. Finally, in addition to serving at the behest of four US presidents, Greenspan in his late tenure **implicitly and explicitly backed** the various "creative financing" mortgage products of the day -- total lunacy, as it turns out! How could a man so well-spoken, with so much expertise, experience, and gravitas get it so wrong?

Securities and Exchange Commission, Commissioner Christopher Cox: As head of the SEC, he governed an era of recklessness and irresponsibility. During his tenure he oversaw critical adjustments in trading (nuances) adopted by the US equities markets, which are credited with **exacerbating volatility** in the markets, and are seen as having contributed to overall increased risk in the marketplace. For instance, during his reign as SEC chief the up-tick rule for short sellers was suspended, in addition to new rules imposed allowing for virtually unlimited borrowing of stock (taken full advantage of by short sellers), which helped lead to increased volatility in the markets. As top cop, he and his lieutenants were responsible for quashing eight separate reviews of allegations of fraud by the now infamous Ponzi scheme racketeer Bernie Madoff. With Mr. Cox at the helm the SEC was ineffective at best, and at worst thoroughly incompetent.

Senator Phil Graham: Known by some as the "high priest" of de-regulation," Senator Phil Graham authored the bill that gutted the Glass-Steagal Act -- a law previously enacted just after the Great Depression designed to prevent financial malpractice and abuse. Rescission of this bill directly led to the merging of banks and brokerage houses, which ultimately helped lead the financial industry's metamorphosis into giant casinos. Republicans, as a rule associated with being the party known for smaller government and fiscal conservatism, experienced a major lapse in judgment, rejecting their historic mantra while betting everything instead on #9, red!?

Treasury Secretary Henry Paulson: Early in the new millennium, while working at Wall Street brokerage Goldman Sachs, he successfully led a lobby to allow for an increase in margin/leverage (caps) at bank/brokerages from the then current 12 to 1 ratio to approximately 30 to 1. Well-educated and an otherwise fine aristocrat working at the pinnacle of the banking world, what could possibly have allowed him (other than an uncompromising greed for higher profits) to disregard any semblance of fiscally responsible investing, and instead adopt a policy of **risk-taking** that would lead his brokerage and others to wager the proverbial farm? (He was smart enough to decipher the difference between investing and flat-out gambling…'ya think?)

Regrettably, his misguided but successful lobby of Washington led to historic changes for US brokerage firms, which directly led to unprecedented leverage in the financial system, which in turn led to the annihilation of the world of finance as we've known it. Remember the proverb "<u>greed leads to even more greed, eventually turning to psychosis and insanity</u>"? (Okay, that's not a real proverb, but you get the point.) As history will no doubt reflect, not more than a handful of years after the above changes went into effect, Wall Street itself <u>collapsed under the weight of debt, deleveraging, and insolvency.</u> (During Wall Street's *"end times,"* Lehman Brothers at its respective high was "levered up" over 40 to 1, Bear Stearns nearly 50 to 1, insurer AIG 65-70 to 1; government mortgage entities Fannie Mae and Freddie Mac were levered 75 to 1 and more than 90 to 1 at their respective highs.) **Translation:** As highly leveraged as many of Wall Street's brokerages were, a few percentage point move by the markets in the opposite direction of a firm's bets would spell <u>total disaster</u>, causing them (nearly instantaneously) to be <u>WIPED OUT</u>! (Thus fell our once cherished, prize, financial behemoths and pillars of world finance.)

Current Federal Reserve Chairman Ben Bernanke: Early in his tenure as Federal Reserve Chairman he was either absolutely <u>clueless</u> as to the extent/depth of the financial tsunami that was building beneath our feet, or he deliberately made erroneous statements in an effort to downplay the economic threat we were facing, at one point labeling the sub-prime mortgage meltdown an "<u>isolated problem</u>"! He was very late in responding to the proverbial writing on the wall that would no doubt have been **blaring out to him** at the time, **telling him that the American economy was on the <u>precipice of collapse.</u>** Without causing a widespread panic in the markets, he could have tried to make more <u>responsible</u> and <u>tempered</u> statements regarding the economy, helping to promote a more cautious posture by investors, shareholders, and retirees with regard to their investments. His current monetary policy of currency devaluation and monetizing debt to fight deflation (as Jim Rogers puts it "printing money until we run out of trees") is **dangerous** policy with far-reaching unintended consequences. (At a minimum, this policy raises the specter of inflation; at worst it could lead to a gross, wholesale devaluation of the US dollar, and hyperinflation.)

3

AMERICAN CAPITALISM GONE WILD
GREED, RECKLESSNESS, AND CORRUPTION PERMEATE WALL STREET

The chickens come home to roost...partners in culpability

Wall Street executives: Imagine the turn of events...some in the very crowd with seemingly unlimited power and privilege running Wall Street just a few years back are today (those who are still left) largely discredited, and at the mercy of massive taxpayer bailouts in the wake of the historic collapse of Wall Street. After having "cleaned up" in recent years, staging record profits while the going was good, ratcheting up their bets and risk in the process (often through use of the derivatives market), Wall Street sounded a death knell the moment markets began to turn significantly lower.

Its prominent CEOs, as well as many of the most powerful and influential bankers in the world -- an elite group of "brainiacs," and cream of the crop (graduates from prestigious Harvard Business School, Yale School of Management, and Wharton School of Finance, to name a few), in a mad quest to maximize profits and returns, leveraged their companies to the point where they became catastrophically unprepared to weather even a slight downturn in the markets. These executives, power players and so-called "gurus" (experts) succumbed to their thirst for greed, violating the time-honored mantra of **smart and responsible investing** which states that one should risk only as much capital as one is willing to part with, and/or take on only enough volatility as he/she is able to ride out (one must anticipate occasional downturns in the market). Additionally, to the great chagrin of the public, Wall Street's CEOs (as well as other prominent corporate CEOs) vis-à-vis salaries and stock compensation packages continued to earn handsomely -- often to the tune of tens of millions of dollars per year -- while their respective companies death spiraled. On the flip side, taking it on the chin, were the aforementioned corporations' and firms' employees, shareholders, and investors, the tax-paying public, and local economies (or in some instances the macro economy). By grossly mismanaging their companies to the point of necessitating taxpayer bailouts, while loading their own pockets whether or not the going was good -- Wall Street's CEOs and others in similar positions of responsibility have earned the ire of the world and have helped put America and the world on the brink of an economic dark age.

Most **financial planners** of all stripes did no better at predicting the carnage that would soon befall the markets, nor were they able to protect their clients' investments. How could they? Typically most make their living by commission, peddling and selling various financial products ("selling" being the operative word). They aren't in the habit of benefiting in any measurable way by instructing their clients to **sell out of their positions** or by recommending their clients exit the overall market. To be sure, well-versed on specific stocks, bonds, and financial products, the whole lot (hindsight tells us) maintained an extremely incompetent and narrow view of the economy. Showing their naïveté and lack of market savvy, many young financial planners, green behind the ears, possessed an inadequate understanding of historic market trends (most basing their market assessments on recent market performance -- the past 10-15 years or so). Lacking historical perspective as well as never having fully conceived of, let alone having personally experienced protracted bear market conditions, young inexperienced financial planners led many an investor astray, straight down a path to the poorhouse. (Whether or not a great many brokers had personally lived through a major period of <u>credit contraction</u> in their lifetime does not mean that they should have been **immune to the concept**.)

My personal view is that if someone is to have credibility as a financial advisor/economic or market analyst or prognosticator, he must be able to view current stock market performance in context of <u>historical data</u> -- that is to say, have a solid understanding of market price action from the most recent 85-100 plus years (at a minimum) and be well versed in major historic market trends (bull/bear). It goes without saying that **history has shown a nasty habit of repeating itself**. Due diligence in current market analysis with a bent on historical perspective and an objective examination of past US stock market performance is what's needed to make basic market prognostications with a degree of accuracy. Only after such training has been thoroughly absorbed by a prospective financial planner should he/she be in the business of advising clients. Lacking a seasoned view of the markets, operating with youthful blinders on (add to this a dose or two of GREED), and you have the basis for financial advisors to be <u>totally dissociated from basic market rationale</u>. The damage caused by this crowd has led to a degree of incalculable suffering throughout the world.

Credit Ratings Agencies -- Mcgraw-Hill Companies Inc. S&P Division (Standard & Poor's), Moody's, Fitch, etc.: History will record these companies as accomplices in Wall Street's scams and corruption. Their reporting in recent years was at best faulty, and at worst, deliberately untruthful and conspiratorial. The evidence points to their <u>routinely</u> glossing over structural and fundamental weaknesses in corporate, banking, structured finance, and sovereign debt balance sheets, and bonds, which they were entrusted to rate, often disregarding or downplaying a company's exposure to toxic, "level 3" assets, liabilities, and/or other critical information such as capitalization rates. Bestowing their highest "AAA" credit ratings on corporate bonds, and other financial instruments when these ratings were completely unjustified (prescribing "AAA" ratings to in-effect worthless paper) directly led to a wholesale ambushing of investors from around the world who put their trust in the rating agencies and their analysis.

While a layperson (or typical individual investor) might not be privy to all the latest breaking news and market updates surrounding publicly traded companies, ratings agencies had a fiduciary responsibility to be on top of all pertinent developments regarding publicly traded companies and other financial instruments. To simply excuse them as being unaware of systemic risks affecting individual corporations, banks, as well as the broader markets until after the fact is disingenuous and an abomination. During the height of the boom, ratings agencies pulled in record profits -- a bulk of their earnings being generated from their roles as advisors in the packaging of hapless C.D.O.s and other (now failed) financial instruments, as well as being directly hired and paid by companies to assess credit risk. (*Can you say conflict of interest?*) Consequently, a political fervor is building in terms of holding rating agencies civilly, even criminally liable for their brazenness in prescribing triple A credit ratings to risky, lackluster, volatile, or financially unsound companies and other suspect financial products. Those having gone belly up or having been "deep sixed" as a result of holding worthless paper (Americans and foreign investors alike) are now increasingly demanding **acknowledgement of culpability by ratings agencies for their perceived willful negligence.**

Other corporate executives led their companies astray -- some just to the brink of insolvency, others directly into bankruptcy court: Top administrators from our nation's companies and corporations (large and small) are instilled with a duty and responsibility to determine and measure all potential risks that may negatively impact their companies -- from both a microeconomic and macroeconomic perspective -- and in the process forge a proper roadmap for their companies' futures. There is no higher priority for an executive than to preserve and protect his/her company from harm, to navigate the company with an even keel, <u>limiting liabilities while maximizing profits</u>. Put in another way, just as physicians take the Hippocratic Oath promising not only to <u>heal</u> but (in the first place) <u>do no harm to the patient,</u> company executives need to reflect a similar mindset. As such, taking pre-emptive action **ahead of** the financial tsunami as it approached, taking all prudent and necessary steps to downsize their companies, reduce risk, shore up balance sheets, "de-lever," etc. should have been the **rule of thumb**.

What actually transpired is quite a different story, however. Top company brass during the early days of the economic fallout as a rule showed a thorough lack of preparedness. (Just look at the median drop in company earnings…need I say more?) Instead of meeting the onset of the global pandemic economic crisis head on, the majority of executives were (like a deer caught in the headlights of an oncoming car) incapacitated into inaction, still unsure whether or not to rock the proverbial boat of economic expansion to the great detriment of their respective companies.

Leading the first wave of corporate bankruptcies/institutions requiring bailouts and other corporate casualties…

…banking institutions/brokerages Countrywide Mortgage, Indymac Bank, Washington Mutual, Lehman Brothers, Morgan Stanley, JP Morgan, Goldman Sachs, Bear Stearns, Fannie Mae, Freddie Mac, Citigroup, Bank of America, Wachovia Bank, PNC Bank, Franklin Bank Corp., Netbank, Banco Popular, the list goes on and on; retailers Circuit City, Foot Locker, Linens and Things, Fortunoff, Filene's Basement, KB Toys, National Wholesale Liquidators; automotive giants GM and Chrysler; insurer AIG; restaurant chains Bennigan's, Steak and Ale, as well as Tavern on the Green; publications Reader's Digest and Playboy magazine; **Teetering on the brink and/or losing money hand over fist…**

homebuilders Pulte, Centex, Lennar, Hovnavian, Beazer, KB Homes; cruise ship operator Royal Caribbean, casino operator MGM Grand, et al. The basic market tenet of ever-repeating economic cycles holds that there are periods of business expansion juxtaposed with periods of economic contraction. Those who understood this simple principle and took steps to adjust their business models preemptively are two legs up on their competition today.

Post-mortem...

Alas, it is not possible to discuss the topic of greed, recklessness, and corruption on Wall Street without giving an honorable mention to the poster child himself, Bernie Madoff. During some of the darkest days of the stock market plunge of late 2008, the public began to get wind of a developing story regarding a record 65-billion-dollar Ponzi scheme involving the bankrupting of whole generations of charities as well as others personally invested with him. With a total disregard for those affected, Bernie Madoff, operating under the nose of authorities went about year in and year out deeply enriching his own pockets as well as those of his lieutenants at the absolute crushing expense of clients and investors. The sheer scope of his crime is so extraordinary that it makes all previous notorious white collar criminals the likes of former MCI Chairman Bernie Ebbers, Tyco CEO Koslowski, and Enron's Jeffrey K. Skilling look like Boy Scouts. What little investor confidence was left as the end of 2008 neared was sapped away by the unfolding allegations of the Bernie Madoff saga. Mr. Madoff embodies one of the most extreme examples of greed in human history and serves as the proverbial icing on the cake to a most bleak chapter of **American capitalism gone wild.**

4

THE PERFECT STORM
MAJOR POLITICAL, ECONOMIC, AND SOCIETAL HEADWINDS, AND THREATS TO AMERICA'S CONTINUED DOMINANCE IN THE WORLD, PLUS PRINCIPAL FACTORS LEADING TO A PRECIPITOUS DECLINE OF THE AMERICAN EMPIRE

One or two factors by themselves would not likely deal a knockout blow to the American Empire, but an overwhelming and nearly simultaneous convergence of numerous factors outlined here provide an historic threat to Uncle Sam's monopoly on world power:

For a country known symbolically for hope, freedom, and optimism throughout the world -- projecting an image of streets paved in gold -- many of the factors listed below represent incontrovertibly damning developments:

1) Erosion of American prestige and popularity throughout the world
2) Erosion of American influence in the world
3) Loss of worldwide confidence in the United States as titular head and leader of global capitalism; America is no longer perceived as a knight in white shining armor, riding to the rescue of other economically challenged nation states, but rather as a nation facing dire economic troubles

itself, requiring massive financial assistance and bailouts. Uncle Sam, despite his best efforts, continues to be largely unable to stem the tide of a <u>global deflationary tsunami</u> that rests squarely upon his citizens.

4) <u>The United States-led brand of capitalism</u> is progressively and increasingly seen as a <u>corrupt, immoral, and bankrupt political and economic system</u>.

5) <u>Increasing numbers of direct</u> and <u>indirect challenges</u> to American political, economic, and military dominance of a so-called "unipolar" world: Countries such as Russia, China, Iran, Venezuela, et al. continue to jockey for a larger role in regional/global politics. It's safe to say, America's enemies <u>smell blood</u>.

6) America appears destined for a long, <u>costly</u>, drawn-out war with Al-Qaida and terrorism in general.

7) A <u>failed, largely insolvent, and thoroughly discredited US banking system</u>: the US banking sector is seen as the <u>author</u> and <u>perpetrator</u> of the global credit crunch and falling real estate valuations, as well as imploding equity indexes and global deflation. American banks kicked off the global contraction in flow of credit, the so-called "<u>life blood</u>" of all economies.

8) A global <u>crisis of confidence</u> continues to emerge regarding US financial assets: <u>securities, US currency, real estate, and various financial products; and now, increasingly, the US treasury bond market</u>. Most recently, China, the US's largest creditor, has reversed a long-standing policy of US treasury purchases and has intimated that it may continue buying treasuries only if certain conditions are attached (and met).

9) The recent <u>collapse</u> of <u>US equity markets</u> and American "inspired" global equity markets

10) The <u>collapse</u> of <u>Wall Street</u>: Wall Street survived, even thrived for years after taking a direct hit and crushing blow

on 9/11. Yet it could not withstand an assault from the 2008 global deflationary tsunami, folding like a deck of cards.

11) Implosion of the US residential housing market due to an historic unwinding in the run-up in prices and massive buildup of inventory -- the larger the boom and the excesses created, the greater the bust

12) The simultaneous collapse of an entire cross-section of American industries: banking, investment, retail, homebuilding, auto, manufacturing, transportation, etc.

13) The progressive eroding value and eroding popularity of the US dollar (current world reserve currency)

14) An overextended, over-indebted, increasingly unemployed American consumer (often insolvent or flirting with insolvency), unable and/or unwilling to afford/manage/maintain his/her usual lifestyle and/or possessions. Increasingly, Americans are falling prey to "upside down" homes (homes where the mortgage amount exceeds the value of the home), unaffordable cars/car loans, unaffordable second homes and college tuitions, falling discretionary spending, etc.

15) Overleveraged, undercapitalized small business owners on the brink, fighting for survival in a failing economy

16) Collapsing commercial real estate valuations and rents; explosion of new vacancies.

17) Skyrocketing federal budget deficits (trillions of dollars per year) with no end in sight. America is the largest debtor nation in the history of the world and growing more indebted by the minute. Our total federal debt burden currently stands at over thirteen trillion dollars. The pace of borrowing has recently climaxed as we have more than doubled our national debt in the past year and a half, adding more debt in this time frame than in the previous 230 years combined.

18) Skyrocketing federal trade deficits (billions of dollars per

year) with no end in sight
19) Collapsing federal, state, and local tax revenues due to a severely contracting economy
20) Deleveraging/unwinding of a 650-700-trillion-dollar global derivatives bubble, a product termed by Warren Buffet as "financial weapons of mass destruction"
21) A massive treasury bond market bubble -- sporting short term yields of near 0%!
22) Unfunded liabilities by the federal government (Social Security, Medicare, Medicaid, etc.) conservatively estimated at some 70-75 trillion dollars (some have the total as high as 106 trillion), and growing rapidly; The Fed's own Social Security and Medicare Board of Trustees acknowledge that the projected long-run program costs are "not sustainable."
23) A rapidly aging baby boom generation as a backdrop to our financial landscape: A tectonic shift is underway in our job market which is likely to structurally weaken our economy for the next few decades, as retiring "baby boomers" switch from their respective roles as local, state, and federal government revenue producers to requiring local, state, and federal subsidies.
24) Progressive loss of the US manufacturing base, a now long-standing trend that has America trading her self-determination, economic independence, and sovereignty -- as well as her long-term economic health -- for higher profit margins and inexpensively produced products from around the world.
25) Burgeoning military commitments throughout the world: The US, in addition to maintaining nearly 800 military bases throughout the world, is at present actively fighting three wars -- one in Afghanistan and another in Iraq, as well as a global War on Terror.
26) The secular bull market in China: The meteoric rise of a

THE PERFECT STORM

rapidly expanding (Red) Chinese economy, one which only recently assumed the coveted #2 position from Japan as the world's second largest economy. In time, China, a nation of 1.4 billion strong, blessed with a strong work ethic as well as a fire and determination to take her (perceived) rightful leadership role among nations, poses a legitimate challenge to our world economic superiority. (Incidentally, China today remains fiscally sound and is the largest creditor nation on earth.)

27) A resurgent Russia with imperial ambitions is superbly positioned to benefit economically during an inflationary or hyperinflationary period which I believe lies ahead.

28) America's continued over-dependence on oil: Most of the world's oil reserves are held by nations and regimes less than friendly (in many instances openly hostile) to America and her allies.

29) Gaping holes in homeland security by virtue of wide open, unsecure, and unprotected borders. (The state of our economy is at present very weak and fragile; a major terrorist attack now would likely serve to completely overwhelm it.)

30) An imminent showdown with Iran on "nukes"; each day brings increasing odds of a new war in the Gulf.

31) The threat of future terrorist attacks, especially those involving weapons of mass destruction

32) A precipitous moral decline: loss of civility, heightened criminality, loss of cherished traditional values.

33) A precipitously declining educational system

34) Gang violence as epidemic: A systemically and systematically growing gang culture in America.

35) Insolvent States of America: Numerous state (and local) governments hemorrhaging money (California, New York, New Jersey, and Michigan to name a few); budgets in shambles, with budget gaps as far as the eye can see.

36) Historic precedent for <u>reversion to the mean -- bubbles, historically speaking, never "pop" or correct only halfway.</u>
37) Death by asphyxiation: "Status quo" remains supreme in Washington. Many of the same politicians in Washington -- "insiders" who ran Uncle Sam into the ground, right up to the very precipice of financial Armageddon -- expect us to have faith and show confidence (against all logic) in our government's ability to fix the plethora of problems and ills plaguing our nation today.
38) <u>Necessary evil: prospective budgetary reforms in Washington and elsewhere.</u> Removal and/or retraction of recent government stimulus packages, bailouts, and guarantees (a foregone certainty with major Republican congressional pick-ups expected in the fall 2010 elections) could in the interim exacerbate the faltering US economy and markets.
39) Thousands of US banks remain vulnerable, undercapitalized, laden with toxic debt, and/or prone to failure, as prospects for further implosions in US residential and commercial real estate markets continue to loom.
40) China's economy (one of a handful of large, fast-growing economies in the world) credited for helping to prop up an otherwise contracting global economy has now begun showing signs of stress and overheating compliments of a real estate mania/bubble the likes of which have rarely been seen, according to famed hedge fund manager Jim Chanos. (China however, still remains in a long term secular bull market.)
41) The growing specter of European sovereign debt defaults (in the "PIGS" nations -- Portugal, Italy/Ireland, Greece, Spain as well as Ukraine, Great Britain, et al.).

5

AMERICAN EMPIRE IN TROUBLE
EERIE SIMILARITIES TO THE COLLAPSE OF THE SOVIET UNION, PLUS
A stark depiction of Uncle Sam's troubles as expressed through the eyes of the Johnson family -- a hypothetical, archetypal family on a downward financial spiral.

Can you remember the day when a principal geo-political player and world superpower **spent incessantly beyond its means year in year out, running up painful deficits for decades on end** -- growing its military budget into perpetuity, funding an arms race, over-reaching militarily (simultaneously running military incursions on multiple continents), continuously expanding military bases (and by extension its military dominance) throughout the world until suddenly one day...poof, it was no longer? Do you remember a time when a leading world power mishandled its economic affairs, misallocating federal funds to such an extent that in the process it deprived its own people of much-needed repairs to domestic infrastructure and critical updates to its economy, running budget deficits as far as the eye could see, progressively falling behind in its commitments to entitlement programs/government pensions etc. until one day it simply ceased to exist? Do you remember the circumstances in which its leaders claimed they did not see an economic collapse brewing until it was too late? Do you remember when a certain government's politicians lacked the fortitude and vision in making the painful, but essential adjustments to their economy in order to <u>put their country</u>

on a path of fiscal responsibility and sustainable economic growth until it was too late? Do you recall the deep state of moral and social decay the country suffered from for years on end before excessive corruption and greed finally helped bring down the empire?

Well, unfortunately, for those of us living in America today, I wasn't describing the Soviet Union of yesteryear, I was referencing gross mismanagement, as well as governmental shortcomings in the good ol' US of A. The similarities between the two powers are frightening, the parallels eerie. The clock continues to tick down, further closing the proverbial door, and lessening our ability to reconcile our ways, balance our books, mend our broken budgets, etc. There is not an abundance of time left in which to turn things around or face similar prospects and a similar fate to that of the **former** Soviet Empire.

To illustrate the nature of Uncle Sam's desperate, overextended, sorry state of affairs, I present to you (as metaphor) the Johnson family…(Uncle Sam as living vicariously through the Johnson family):

The Johnson family, needless to say, is heavily in debt, having recently completed the purchase of a 6,500 square foot "McMansion" home (a home that for all intents and purposes they cannot afford). They are leasing two brand new cars which cost about $800 per month to finance. Just like everyone else around them, they are struggling more and more as the economy around them continues to deteriorate. The Mrs. recently lost her job and they have now fallen to a single household income. In fact, their budgets show a negative cash flow as far as the eye can see -- unless they are (somehow miraculously) able to land a 2nd job in the household. They have borrowed, and borrowed, and borrowed again and they are leveraged to the hilt. Now, after unsuccessfully petitioning their lender for additional moneys over a period of some months, and having ended up instead borrowing from friends and family alike, they find themselves in <u>foreclosure,</u> unable to make their monthly payments on their home or their lofty real estate tax payments. In fact, they barely have enough money to keep the most critical utilities active, and all non-essential services have already been cut. Compounding matters, just a few days ago they received a notice in the mail stating that their cars are about to be repossessed.

Enter neighbor Mr. Ben Bernanke, who concocts a financial scheme by which the Johnsons are able to borrow a jumbo personal loan -- nearly half a million dollars (even though the Johnsons cannot afford to pay the loans they have at present). Ben claims that they will be able to stretch their payments out indefinitely (emphasizing "<u>indefinitely</u>"). He stipulates that once the loan is paid off, total payments (principal and interest) will cost north of 8 million dollars, but he assures them that (in his opinion as <u>close</u> <u>personal</u> <u>friend</u> and also as a <u>trained</u> <u>financial</u> <u>advisor</u>) they simply have no choice at this point. Not satisfied that he has done all that he can to alleviate the Johnson family's stress, Mr. Bernanke talks the Johnsons into running a counterfeit printing press right out of their garage whereby they will literally gain a capacity to print money out of thin air. (Desperate times call for desperate measures!)

Now, after a few reams of paper and a few clicks of the print button, the Johnsons begin to breathe a new sigh of relief, having just brought all their bills up to date as well as getting the majority of creditors off their backs. However, the Johnsons recognize that they are still (for some reason) being treated <u>rather standoffishly</u> by almost everyone. Their creditors continue to remain quite jittery and rather suspicious as to the Johnson family's abrupt change in fortune. The tax man is in the process of preparing an audit. For some reason, no one deep down believes that the Johnsons will be able to <u>maintain or sustain their current lifestyle and future payments in the long run</u>. In sum, aside from their recent display of "feats of magic," most around them still remain unimpressed by the Johnsons, believing instead that the Johnsons likely gained their new status by virtue of some sort of <u>ploy</u> or <u>scam</u>.

◄ 21ST CENTURY GREAT GLOBAL DEPRESSION

The moral of the story...

The desperate measures taken by the Johnson family are likely to still end up being in vain, adding insult to injury, and in the end actually serve to compound their problems. In addition to the prospects of losing their various possessions, the Johnsons (once the law catches up to them) are likely to face a battalion of criminal charges including federal bank fraud and racketeering charges, as well as a slew of other federal counterfeiting and forgery charges. As such, the Johnsons now face the prospect of not only losing all their worldly possessions but also their dignity, their reputation, and their personal freedoms in the process.

In hindsight, it would have been better had they tucked their proverbial tails between their legs and taken immediate steps to begin the process of **living within their means,** saving whatever dignity they had left in going about the business of trying to rebuild their lives. Declaring bankruptcy in the early stages of default would at the very least have kept the Johnsons out of jail, sparing their marriage in the process. Who knows -- with some luck they might even have been able to restructure their home mortgage to the point of retaining their home. Now we will never know for sure. "Staying in the game" (battling on/going for broke!) a slogan often used by Mad Money host Jim Cramer to entice his viewers to show no retreat, would have equated to profoundly <u>unsound advice</u> for the Johnsons, to say the least. While there is a time to "shoot for the stars" there is also a time for pause, reflection, retrenchment, and rebuilding. **The bible tells us...to everything, there is a season.**

6

OUR "UPSIDE DOWN" WORLD
A GLOBAL COMMUNITY OF NATIONS FLAT BROKE PLUS DIRE CONSEQUENCES OF ENTITLEMENT PROGRAMS GOING BUST

The greatest era of wealth creation in human history as tied to the Age of Bubbles...

Please review the following information obtained from a recent posting on MSN.com which lists the <u>largest debtor nations in the world</u>. The following list rates countries based on their ratio of <u>total debt</u> as compared to <u>gross domestic product</u>. In essence, the following statistics show us each nation's ability to pay back their debt as based on total annual revenue collected. For example, Ireland, which tops the list, would require more than 8 years of total gross federal revenue -- using today's G.D.P. calculations -- just to pay back the principal on debt owed 1) Ireland 811% 2) United Kingdom 336% 3) Belgium 327% 4) Hong Kong 295% 5) Netherlands 268% 6) Switzerland 264% 7) Austria 191% 8) France 168% 9) Denmark 159% 10) Germany 137.5% 11) Spain 137% 12) Sweden 129% 13) Finland 116% 14) Norway 111% 15) The United States 95%.

With the exception of Hong Kong, this list of the world's most indebted nations reads like a *Who's Who* of the West. The United States, along with a smattering of economies in Eurozone (and

Japan) account for roughly 80% of world G.D.P. and are flat-out broke, growing more indebted by the second.

Future ramifications for debtor nations...

When all is said and done, countries will be affected to differing degrees by the 21ˢᵗ Century Great Global Depression as based upon each individual country's underlying fiscal strength. Initially (as we have witnessed in the recent past), most major economies (and emerging markets) will decline hand in hand, absorbing a crashing world economy shoulder to shoulder. However, it is likely that after a period of time, today's fast-growing economies in the developing world are likely to focus all the more internally for growth, spurring <u>internal consumer demand,</u> and thus allowing them to fare **disproportionately better** than today's slow-growing mature economies (typically debtor nations laden with **inescapable debt).** Today's western nations, G7 and others, in addition to having to surmount <u>crippling levels of debt,</u> are laden with budget deficits often rivaling their G.D.P.s or in some instances surpassing their G.D.P. by a wide margin (see above list). These nations are likely to fare **disproportionately worse over the long haul.**

Regarding America's debt levels; a few words on the overall financial health of the American consumer...

A candid look at the fiscal underpinnings of most Americans/American families reveals the majority owning **<u>virtually none</u> or <u>no assets at all</u>**. The combination of owning negligible assets while owing (in aggregate) $70,000 (a consequence of Americans' federal and personal debt load), leaves most Americans **"upside down"** (a real estate reference denoting <u>negative equity</u>). **Here are the numbers:** A typical US citizen owes more than $40,000 just to our federal debt burden alone as new debt and interest continues to accrue daily. In addition, the average American citizen today holds approximately

OUR "UPSIDE DOWN" WORLD ➤

$9,000 in credit card debt as well as (roughly) $20,000 in auto and/or school loans, personal loans, as well as (in many instances) back-owed utility bills, medical bills, child support payments, etc. The total debt load of $70,000 rises impressively when mortgage debt is factored in especially for the nearly 12 million Americans upside down on their homes (a figure which is rising rapidly). As such, <u>many Americans should be so lucky to be</u> **FLAT BROKE.** Taking this financial analysis one step further, an argument can be made which states **the poor living in the Third World today -- with just the proverbial shirts on their backs -- are** <u>wealthier</u> **than the average American.** Sad but true.

As to our "unfunded liabilities" quagmire, a candid look at debt-laden US especially in regard to our seismically dysfunctional and growing-rapidly-defunct entitlement programs...

Although we score 15th place overall based on the outstanding debt to G.D.P. (gross domestic product) model, the US maintains the <u>unenviable position</u> of being the <u>most indebted nation on earth,</u> or more precisely the **most indebted nation in the history of the world,** owing (at present) more than 13 trillion dollars. (Our nation pays more than 3 billion dollars per day in interest alone.) In addition this **doesn't even begin to sum up our total overall indebtedness**.

Adding to the widely recognized, ever-exploding/skyrocketing national debt load, Uncle Sam is up to his neck in so-called **"unfunded liabilities"** (deficits/"uncollected" moneys owed to entitlement programs -- Social Security, Medicare, and Medicaid, as well as government pension plans). These programs are effectively insolvent today and are headed to <u>oblivion</u> barring massive cutbacks and reform (Medicare is projected to begin a net negative cash flow by 2015; Social Security as early as 2010). This <u>fiasco</u> -- some refer to it as a shell game or pyramid scheme -- has Uncle Sam on the hook for an additional 70-106+ trillion dollars of obligations

35 ➤

depending on your accounting (that's trillion with a "t"). Adding the two sums together (federal deficit and unfunded liabilities) we arrive at a grand total of no less than **82 trillion dollars** of tangible, crippling indebtedness, even though many of the debts are arguably not due *all at once*. Even worse? Our current **federal budget deficits are projected to reach a staggering 4.5 to 6+ trillion dollars per year over the coming decade** (a combination of roughly 1.5 to 2 trillion dollar annual budget shortfalls in addition to more than 3.5 trillion yearly in unfunded liabilities). **Thus, over the coming decade, we are due to reach a sum of 130-155 trillion dollars of crippling debt.** Federal budget deficits as well as overall federal debt are likely to climb even further if our economic troubles persist and/or tax revenues continue their historic plunge.

Back to the US consumer for a moment...

If one were to calculate 70 trillion dollars in unfunded liabilities (a conservative estimate) and divide this figure by 310 million (roughly America's population today), we arrive at a sum of more than $225,000 of additional debt carried by each and every American citizen. Finally, if we were to combine the two sums: $225,000 and our previous sum of $70,000 (a combination of federal and personal debt), we arrive at a staggering grand sum of $295,000 of debt -- owed by each and every American alive today.

One final ominous mind-boggling statistic: Due to the combination of precipitously rising federal indebtedness and falling overall US net worth (which now stands at 51.9 trillion dollars as compared to a recent high of 64 trillion), we (as a nation) have become technically "upside down," with potential to fall further upside down in a mad hurry.

...that this nation, under God, shall have a new birth of... insolvency*? What? No way! Could this really be happening? So what's a country to do?*

OUR "UPSIDE DOWN" WORLD

This need not be our destiny so long as we find the <u>courage</u> and <u>fortitude</u> to make the necessary budgetary reforms now. The burning question at hand…*will we take the historic steps in bringing our fiscal house in order, or will we wait for cascading debt defaults in Europe to pave the way for our own debt default troubles? Will we muster up enough will and patriotism to lead a charge for the hearts and minds of Americans -- a plea for fiscal sanity -- or will we sanction the transformation of our nation into the* **<u>Insolvent States of America?</u>** The choice is ours, and ours alone. Keep in mind, <u>sound</u> and <u>solvent</u> federal, state, and local governments, individual, and corporate **fiscal houses**, the backbone of the American empire, are necessary for us to <u>maintain</u> and <u>retain</u> our way of life.

In closing, let me project the best possible scenario for our ailing economy, the one true magic elixir, **sustainable economic growth.** *(Imagine a <u>remedy without a plethora of side effects</u> of the kind experienced as a result of excessive money printing, the creation of new asset and credit bubbles, excessive bailouts, and/or massive federal spending?)* Sadly however, this "fix" appears elusive, and even if it were to occur or if we could rely on prosperous economic times ahead, servicing our enormous debt burden will take a <u>long time</u> and will be <u>costly.</u> **<u>The perfect economic storm</u> -- a combination of strong economic headwinds, massive deflation, contracting credit, escalating debt levels, rising unemployment, and a rising interest rate environment, as well as escalating tax burdens, virtually ensures no quick turnaround for the global economy.**

7

BITING OFF MORE THAN IT CAN CHEW
GOVERNMENT AGENCIES AND PROGRAMS ALREADY RUN INTO THE GROUND ATOP NEW PRECIPITOUSLY GROWING OBLIGATIONS

Shall we ever again be graced with the disposition, optimism, as well as circumstances to do as Maya Angelou intimated in William Jefferson Clinton's inaugural poem in 1992?
On the pulse of this new day
You may have the grace to look up and out
And into your sister's eyes, into
Your brother's face, your country
And say simply
Very simply
With hope
Good morning.
…or will we, together with our offspring and countless generations thereafter, spend every waking hour of every day working incessantly to remediate the mistakes of our cumulative past, slaving away to pay interest on moneys borrowed 50, 75, or even 100 years previously?

The following **list** represents **US federal government programs/agencies including the federal government itself,** that are either <u>operating in the red,</u> <u>totally insolvent</u> and in need of continuous financial bailouts to stay afloat, <u>heading towards insolvency,</u>

hemorrhaging money, or broke and/or laden with toxic assets:
1) **Fannie Mae** (government backed mortgage provider and insurer -- trillions of dollars injected to stave off collapse; more needed.)
2) **Freddie Mac** (government backed mortgage provider and insurer -- trillions of dollars injected to stave off collapse; more needed.)
3) **Sallie Mae** (student loan provider -- headed for insolvency.)
4) **US Federal Government** (13 trillion dollars in debt, headed to a sum of more than 20 trillion dollars in the next decade alone; federal debt which has doubled in recent years is on course to double yet again.)
5) **Federal Reserve** (central banking system -- "monetizing" debt; holds nearly 1 trillion dollars of toxic paper/assets and guarantees; continues to buy more failed financial instruments such as mortgage backed securities, etc.)
6) **US Treasury** (holds over 1 trillion dollars in toxic paper/assets.)
7) **Social Security** (utterly insolvent -- unfunded liabilities total approximately 30 trillion or more dollars.)
8) **Medicare** (irreparably insolvent -- unfunded liabilities total approximately 40 trillion or more dollars.)
9) **US Postal Service** (in deep fiscal peril, hemorrhaging money.)
10) **FDIC** (flat-broke after 140 takeovers of failed banking institutions in 2009; rate of bank failures continues to increase and is expected to accelerate for years to come.)

Are these numbers real, or are they a mirage? How could deficits of this magnitude invade our once veritably and fundamentally prosperous nation? Is it possible that mismanagement has reached such epic proportions? Why didn't either party (Republicans or Democrats) find the political will to right our sinking economic ship while we still had time? Where were our duly designated *representatives when push came to shove? Does the notion of <u>cost-containment</u> even compute in the minds of our elected officials? How could we allow our noble roots as well as our sensibilities/sense of preservation to be pulverized as a result of complete and total fiscal neglect? How could higher-ups in Washington expose our country to such peril in times of global war, turmoil, and upheaval? I ask, for the love of God...is there a person remaining who actually believes in his or her heart of hearts that our federal government is capable of successfully managing atop its numerous existing obligations (including the ones listed above) the vast bulk of US mortgages, much of our automotive market, many of our largest banking institutions, a new health care system, as well as a formidable part of our insurance industry, etc.? With our Fed's abysmal fiscal track record, can we afford to continue with business as usual in Washington (with not a single budgetary reform to show) and somehow expect better fiscal management and oversight starting today?*

8

THREAT TO CIVILIZATION
<u>DERIVATIVES</u>, THE MOTHER OF ALL TICKING TIME BOMBS; OUR 680 TRILLION DOLLAR GLOBAL CONUNDRUM

Who knew the apocalypse would begin in cyberspace or at trading desks around the world?

"**Financial weapons of mass destruction.**" **So sayeth the Oracle of Omaha, Warren Buffet.** A superbly "dangerous game," **<u>derivatives trading</u>** symbolizes our go-go era of extreme leverage, risk-taking, and in some cases, "betting the farm." I dare say (aside from its use as a hedge against risk/insurance against open trades -- "upside and downside protection") speculative derivatives trading should be called what it is -- <u>gambling</u> in its purest form. Yet brilliantly packaged/marketed just as cigarette commercials of yesteryear, it is sold to the public as an <u>investment/trading</u> vehicle!

To this day minimally regulated, these financial products allow investors to wager bets at pennies on the dollar. For example, buying ten contracts of a simple put or call option might cost you a few thousand dollars, granting you control of 1,000 shares of XYZ company. If (for the sake of argument) the underlying security (stock symbol XYZ) were trading at $100 per share, you would instantly find yourself commanding a $100,000 block of stock. Multiply this ratio on a **grand global trading scale**, including large institutional trading, and you arrive at the kind of <u>extreme, incalculable leverage,</u>

liability, and volatility that nightmares are made of!!!

Particularly worrisome is the fact that many "investors" of all pedigrees from around the globe use the derivatives market as a trading vehicle with dreams of vast profits and massive upside potential, and are often devoid of a full understanding and comprehension of the degree of danger that this market possesses. Choose the right put or call option (not much different from picking the correct number and/or color on a roulette wheel and you can easily double your money the same day, maybe even in the same hour; choose the wrong trade (odds greatly favor this scenario) and watch your "investment" get vaporized.

Intrigued by derivatives and a desire to try it first hand, I briefly delved into derivatives trading. After a few weeks in the marketplace and once the dust had settled, I (by all measures a fairly sophisticated and seasoned investor/trader) realized I had been extremely lucky to get out alive! It was *after* I had closed my last position that I fully recognized the extreme and spectacular leverage I had been exposed to. Even without trading *on margin* I had been placing my highly leveraged trades at only 2-3 cents on the dollar (in other words I was "levered up" nearly 50 to 1!). Brokerage statements arriving in the mail after the fact confirmed what I already knew: All along I had been moving countless millions of dollars using (what amounted to) a very discreet sum of seed money. **My post-trading assessment and conclusion:** Had I ventured to stay in the market for just a few weeks longer, I would have lost 100% of principal and been definitively wiped out!

Recapping from a previous chapter

Do you recall the aggregate debt load that each and every American carries? Remember the $40,000-plus federal debt load held by every man, woman, and child (US citizens) living in America today, and the additional $30,000 plus in personal debt (credit cards, school loans, car loans etc.), plus the additional $225,000 of *unfunded liabilities each of us is responsible for as a consequence of insolvent social services programs?* **Now factor in approximately 1.9 million dollars of risk for every man, woman, and child alive in the world today -- floating around in the dark matter of the global derivatives market -- and you arrive at a grand total of 2.2 million dollars of aggregate debt/risk held by Americans today (<u>a combination of derivatives risk, moneys owed to federal entitlement programs, as well as federal and personal debt loads</u>)!** Now, do you still wonder, as do I, why the "doom and gloom" crowd continues to gets such a bad rap? Furthermore, are you as convinced as before of our prospects for a <u>sustainable recovery</u>?

The facts as I've stated them here are **incontrovertible**. They exist, they are real, and they tell an <u>ominous</u> tale about our soundly broke, insanely "over-leveraged" world just moments after the end of the <u>Great Era of Credit Expansion</u>. These facts are rarely reported on, however, as though by denying their existence they will somehow cease to exist. *Can you imagine the physical insult and carnage to our global financial system that is likely to result from a continued deleveraging and unwinding of a 680-trillion-dollar (some say as high as one quadrillion) derivatives market/bubble alone? Can you envision the potential ensuing fallout on the global economy?*

Keep in mind, our current **global G.D.P.** (gross domestic product) stands at approximately 50-60 trillion dollars. In contrast, the derivatives market sports a capitalization of nearly 700 trillion dollars which (for all intents and purposes) translates to a <u>bubble</u> with a market capitalization of between 12-14 times the size of our current global economy. (In other words, the value of today's derivatives market equals 12-14 years of global G.D.P., the combined economic output from all of the world's nearly 200 nations!) **Conclusion: Make no mistake, the unwinding of this historic bubble, unprecedented in its size and scope in all human history, has the power to just as easily wipe out a billion-dollar company as it does a trillion-dollar economy -- on a dime!** Now try sleeping at night.

9

SOLUTIONS ELUDE US
MODERN AMERICAN SOCIETY RELEGATED TO PETTY PARTISAN BICKERING AND PLAYING THE BLAME GAME

Today's political mantra is party before country. We need solidarity and unity of purpose to meet the avalanche of historic and "generational" crises we currently face…

Hyper-Partisanship has become a scourge upon our society. It has permeated all facets of society -- politics, journalism, television, print media, etc. Scoring points on political adversaries and playing the blame game is the norm; quest for higher ratings reigns supreme. Due to a sustained campaign of partisan rhetoric and "ill will" from both sides in recent years -- compromise and finding commonsense solutions seem to go whoosh…right over most of our heads at this point. Instead of displaying a sense of common purpose to help mitigate a plethora of historic economic, fiscal, and moral crises, we choose instead to fight amongst ourselves, in effect helping to defeat ourselves. Hyper-partisanship and party *arrogance* **must die** before our nation can begin to heal its wounds and ultimately renew itself.

Taking a firm stand on moral issues and standing on one's principles is well within the purview of most, but taking a position which one does not believe in, in his or her heart of hearts, is pathetic, illogical, misguided, immoral, and just plain wrong. Partisanship with the express intent of polarizing dialogue, creating gridlock, dividing instead of uniting, and espousing party allegiance and loyalty before country should be relegated to a domain of fanatics, lunatics, and losers, not mainstream politicians, journalists, or political pundits. Toeing the party line just for the sake of doing so is the **height of despicability**.

In addition, trying to bolster one's party's image at all costs, never accepting blame for any mistakes or mishaps, and diminishing or belittling political opponents is not only hypocritical and crass behavior, but fundamentally dangerous behavior in that it tends to lead to even more arrogant and obstructionist behavior down the road. (Lying is similar in that it often leads to even more intricate lies in an attempt to cover up the original lie.) In so saying, hyper-partisanship is a slippery slope, and once blood has been drawn on either side, it often becomes nearly impossible to instigate a truce between warring political factions.

Unless something changes drastically (and I pray soon) to change our dysfunctional national psyche, we are destined to play the blame game all the way down, contributing in earnest to our miserable circumstances, and accelerating our economic collapse. Expending whatever dwindling amount of resources and national energy we have left in fighting ourselves is not wise. Wasn't it Abraham Lincoln who suggested that a house divided cannot stand? Combining all our resources and national treasure to bear in fighting the economic tsunami heading our way means formulating a sincere political **truce** between Republicans and Democrats: pledging (at all costs) to work in relative harmony to resolve difficult issues, dropping the air of infallibility and work for common solutions in a way that does not involve destroying or demeaning one's political opponents. **This is part and parcel of the way back from the abyss.**

Case in point -- the nightly back and forth on cable TV by ideologues and partisans, between conservative-leaning cable news media and liberal-leaning cable news stations: Though the economic landscape continues to burn **beneath our feet,** you couldn't tell from nightly cable news coverage, which is mired in provocative dialogue, often with the express aim of taking cheap shots at political adversaries, the more flamboyant the better -- (better too for ratings). Given the nature of our troubles today…do we really care who ultimately started our current trajectory to economic collapse, which party screwed up more, or who deserves more blame? Every second that goes by is a second we need not waste if we're sincere in trying to emerge from the current landscape of economic chaos. **The stakes have never been higher; we've got to get this right.** Otherwise it is not inconceivable (nor will it take a "Twilight Zone" delusional experience) to tune in to MSNBC in the not-too-distant future to find the "worst person in the world" segment changed to "Americans, the most broke-assed people on earth," or find an altered version of Fox News' "liberal translation treatment" segment changed to "Americans all, BASP" (bankruptcy asset repossession treatment).

10

CRACKS BEGIN TO APPEAR IN OUR BUBBLE-ECONOMY FOUNDATION
RATE OF IMPLOSION PICKS UP STEAM AS EACH STRUCTURAL WALL GIVES WAY; THE EMPEROR HAS NO CLOTHES!

A chain reaction, beginning with the meltdown of the "sub-prime" mortgage market and crashing of new housing starts, leads to a severe US residential housing correction and lending freeze, which again (directly and indirectly) leads to a host of bank failures and sharp sell-offs in global equity markets, as well as the complete collapse of Wall Street brokerages. Can you say "<u>unsustainable growth</u>"?

Our recent economic expansion was based on at least three (or more) completely <u>unsustainable</u> <u>pillars</u>: 1) <u>a credit bubble based on excessive consumer consumption and spending,</u> 2) a <u>real estate bubble</u> (spawning a vast over-reliance on a single industry/sector for growth -- the US real estate market, and 3) a massive -- never before seen in the history of humanity -- <u>debt bubble</u>. All bubbles virtually <u>simultaneously</u> <u>touched</u> their absolute respective <u>historic peaks, all busting in sync with one another as well</u>. One might argue that a collapse of just one of the main pillars to our economy could have left our economy hobbling along in a garden-variety recession. However, it was the near-simultaneous collapse of all three bubbles/pillars of our makeshift economy that caused our global economy to surge right off a cliff. Now we are left to witness a purging of excesses in a rather **apocalyptic show of massive global economic contraction**.

As far as being able to pinpoint the precise break out and creation of fault lines for the 21st Century Great Global Depression, the crashing and cascading collapse of company earnings, beginning with US homebuilders, comes to mind. If you were looking for ground zero of the economic fallout, you would likely be led on a path directly to July/August 2005 when US homebuilders' fortunes began their abrupt historic reversal. Today, just a few years later, most US homebuilders continue to struggle to survive. (Housing starts are down more than 80% from their respective highs.) The intense collapse of real estate homebuilding stocks signaled a death knell to our mortgage insurance market as well as helped inspire an implosion of our sub-prime mortgage market. Thus began an ominous downward trend in US and global real estate, an ever-tightening spiral of falling real estate prices, deflating real estate revenues and rents, and (in short order) escalating real estate taxes.

A piling on...

Enter a **global credit freeze**; total dislocation of lending markets, and a fast-track **collapse of the US and global banking system**. The consequence of these various events was a creation of deflationary downward pressure on virtually all markets, beginning with the aforementioned global real estate market (less credit in circulation denotes a deflationary environment). As home prices crashed, equity markets corrected and loss of wealth turned palpable; this in turn led to a serious erosion of global consumer (and investor) confidence. Selling begat selling, resulting in equity market "margin calls" (demand by brokers to raise capitalization in accounts that have fallen below the required minimum), deleveraging of investments (reduction of risk), and led to a further precipitous decline in global equities markets. Thus the world (in a New York minute) was forced to walk through fire as the previous mantra-of-the-day, "levering up" (extending risk) was dead, replaced instead by a campaign of massive and historic deleveraging.

The extraordinary and expeditious collapse of Wall Street came next as brokerage house after brokerage house turned insolvent literally overnight. Some of the world's largest and most influential banking institutions collapsed in tandem, their balance sheets similarly stacked with "toxic" un-sellable assets and over-excessive leverage. Unable to borrow in a broken global banking system, the US and global consumer became paralyzed. Flow of credit stalled as credit spigots were shut down. Instantly, consumers were turned away, unable to tap into the so-called housing ATM (cashing out equity with home equity loans, mortgage refinances, etc.), unable to secure much-needed credit for home, auto, personal, and business purposes alike. The corresponding loss of wealth effect resulting from a 40%-45% plummet of total global equity in the period of late 2007-early 2009 wrote the epitaph for consumer spending, RIP late 2007.

More shoes appear poised to drop...

Deflationary monsters of biblical proportions wait on the horizon, preparing to ravage US and global consumers and investors: A further contracting of commercial real estate and credit card/bank card markets as well as an unwinding of the derivatives bubble to name a few. These events accurately represent some of the next legs down in our deflationary trajectory.

All told, our current global consumer spending moratorium has led to an historic collapse in company earnings which has in turn, led to a global unemployment crisis. Now many of the world's largest economies are in freefall, the pace of the decline truly breathtaking. So far, and despite massive and historic intervention by world governments and central banks (especially the US Federal Reserve) to stem the economic slide, results have been no more than measured.

Viewing the prospects for the globe in the best possible light, it is plausible to glean from current circumstances that one day -- likely after much pain and suffering -- new life and vitality will once again begin to sprout in the crushed hull of our global economy, confidence will begin to grow, and new market leaders and industries will be born. Let us hope and pray.

11

THINKING THE PARTY WOULD NEVER END
GETTING CAUGHT IN THE VORTEX OF CREDIT EXPANSION, AMERICANS AND THE WORLD ARE CAUGHT FLAT-FOOTED

Overbuilding, over-expansion, over-capacity rules the day as most industries are caught thoroughly unprepared for a global general buyers' strike. Businesses are faced with a clear choice: Contract or die.

It can be said that during the late stages of the global credit boom/mania both the <u>global consumer</u> and <u>global business community</u> viewed the economic climate with a <u>false sense of optimism,</u> their assets/company balance sheets with a <u>false sense of prosperity,</u> and the markets with a <u>carefree attitude and naïveté,</u> especially related to the final upwardly-catapulting days of the credit boom. (Folks throughout the world were operating with **credit expansion blinders** on -- in full!)

Decisions, for instance, as to whether or not aggressively expand one's business, maintain a status quo or to downsize (a process which often includes laying off workers, shuttering up stores, reducing exposure to certain markets, etc.) are typically made after careful consideration of the <u>economic climate.</u> Once **macroeconomic projections are established,** only then should businesses move to a candid assessment of internal company data in deciding on a proper course of action...*to expand or not to expand.* (As there is a right time and place to expand one's business, there is most certainly a wrong time and a wrong place as well.) The businesses that did not heed the proverbial writing on the wall, disregarding the red flags that were flying in all directions foretelling a superheated economy and an unsustainable boom, typically took no evasive action or necessary precautions as they headed into the belly of the beast (economic storm 2007+). Rather than downsizing, raising cash to meet their respective ever-growing financial obligations, recapitalizing, deleveraging (reducing risk), reducing inventory, etc., many in corporate America as well as numerous unsuspecting individual businessmen and women, entrepreneurs, small business, etc. in fact **expanded** their businesses in 2006 and 2007 when the global macro economy was showing severe signs of stress and destabilization. This cumulative shortsightedness resulted in a brutal trouncing of many businesses, even entire industries and economic sectors, some of which to this day still remain on *life support.*

If you relied on the federal government for guidance in helping you steer straight and avoid major economic pitfalls during these volatile times, you would have been left sorely disappointed. Most Americans got absolutely no warning signals from our government as to the absolute dire condition of our then-faltering economy -- rather, the only routine cues and sound bites coming from Washington were to the effect that "the sub-prime mortgage meltdown is an isolated event," or "the fundamentals of our economy are strong." Thus numerous citizens were led astray believing in the **"soundness"** of our economy when in fact a candid and sober look by virtually anyone -- business owners, corporate brass, investors, shareholders, or retirees -- as to our macroeconomic state of affairs would have shown overwhelmingly that **real estate valuations** were in the stratosphere, that **securities markets'** price/earnings ratios were priced to perfection, that imbalances were growing on a daily basis, and that a historic "correction" in the markets was in order. Telltale signs of a looming market top were everywhere: a **universal**

THINKING THE PARTY WOULD NEVER END

buildup in prices **encompassing virtually all markets and regions of the globe;** never before seen month after month and year after year price growth in real estate; outright mania in lending markets; credit offered "on demand" with lending standards in the crapper; contrarian indicators screaming red flags with bull sentiment hitting the roof, and simultaneous new all-time highs being achieved in numerous global markets concurrently.

Shouldn't this have qualified as a time for pause and reflection, for heeding the infamous "Buffetism" "<u>be greedy when others are fearful and fearful when others are greedy</u>"? Instead, during the "end times" of the credit boom three "D"s ruled the Street: (market) <u>dislocation</u>, (market) <u>dichotomy</u>, and (market) <u>divergence</u>... between deteriorating economic fundamentals on the one hand, and on the other, rapidly advancing market indexes. The warning signs were posted clear for all to see (most chose not to). **As a result, many businesses expanding in the final days of the historic era of credit expansion did so only to contract at an even faster pace once the bubble had burst.**

So what's next?

Where does this leave the majority of us, you ask? A <u>consequence</u> of <u>severe</u> <u>economic contraction/a fallout in G.D.P. (gross domestic product)</u>, <u>deflation,</u> and <u>credit contraction</u> has precipitated falling employment levels, and a contraction of many -- if not most -- of our key industries: **Downsizing** is the new mantra; in light of the violently correcting nature of our current business cycle it's hard to visualize how virtually any industry will be spared.

Excess supply built up during the boom years will have to be "worked off," as rebalancing our rapidly shrinking economy will require us to mitigate and dispense with an overabundance of homes, apartment buildings, condos, beach houses, second homes, McMansions, and waterfront properties. Commercial properties, including numerous malls, office buildings, stores, storefronts, rental space, apartment complexes, and mini malls will have to be closed before all is said and done. Shuttering up boat dealerships, RV dealerships, auto dealerships, motorcycle dealerships, as well as auto parts stores, car washes, and car rental agencies are an essential consequence of excessive supply and/or falling demand. Retailers and retailing chains of all stripes will need to downsize as a glut of shoe stores, clothing stores, furniture stores, fashion accessory stores, crafts stores, electronics stores, toy stores, stationary stores, pet supply stores as well as restaurants, pizza chains, Chinese restaurants, diners, supermarkets, dry cleaners, and laundromats will need to be dramatically reduced as well.

Homebuilders will face a reality check -- either go out of business or be forced to merge with other homebuilders to survive; home improvement centers, lumber yards, plumbing supply houses, electrical supply shops, real estate brokers and agents, mortgage brokers, bankers, and banking institutions will need to contract to meet rapidly falling demand. There's no need for the numerous venture capitalists, financial advisors, financial brokers, banking analysts, business administrators, and managers we have at present. An abundance of wineries, ice cream parlors, churches, gas stations, convenience stores, and fruit markets as well as other businesses built during the boom times are now, sadly, stuck squarely in the mire of overcapacity, and will either strive to survive or be forced to close.

Businesses built on discretionary spending such as travel agencies, cruise ship companies, resorts, hotels, nail parlors, hair salons, coffee shops, movie theaters, bowling alleys and bingo halls, golf courses, mini golf, country clubs, and amusement parks will be required to scale back their operations in a major way or risk an inevitable collapse. For our contracting economy we now exceed our need for the vast number of hospitals, drug stores, airplanes, machine shop technicians, shippers, truckers, tow truck drivers, and mechanics -- businesses and jobs built up during the boom years. Treacherous economic times dictate that we downsize our vastly overbuilt "sin" industries -- casinos, liquor stores, adult industry-related jobs, massage parlors, and XXX stores. Even (sadly) charities will have to be scaled back due to lack of funding. Finally, it goes without saying that a number of magazines, publications, bookstores, print media, and periodicals (already in a perpetual bear market) will need to close. I could go on and on, but I think you get the picture. The painful fundamentals of a severely contracting economy <u>absolutely mandate</u> the <u>gross</u> <u>downsizing</u> of most industries. (Don't hate…I'm just the messenger.)

12

FAST TRACK TO POVERTY
INESCAPABLE CONSEQUENCES OF A DEFLATIONARY DEATH SPIRAL -- ALL ASSET CLASSES ARE PULVERIZED!

A seismic change of fortune is in the offing as the world grows vastly poorer in a hurry. Americans from all walks of life and all socio-economic classes -- especially those contained within the broad spectrum of the "investor class" ("Main Street" to Wall Street, workers with 401K pension plans, retirees with nest eggs, the uber-rich, etc.) -- get slaughtered!

The **big "O"** in context of the Great Global Depression represents a **gigantic "zero"** (all those currently broke), the un-suspecting and ill-prepared of all stripes whose assets have been pulverized: the over-extended, over-leveraged, overly invested, those with obsolete business models, as well as the overly optimistic (investors maintaining an overly bullish stance during an overtly collapsing economy). Now after a precipitous decline in most markets, these same victims litter our streets -- the overwhelmed, overtly bankrupt, obviously insolvent, as well as investors oppressively paralyzed into inaction (or forced to sell at market bottoms), the otherwise unemployed, overly impoverished, and utterly destitute. (I know…I cheated on the last one.)

Let me take a moment to address the **virtually unimaginable, practically apocalyptic wealth destruction** occurring around

the globe of late: As I've stated previously, in a matter of fewer than 18 months (from late 2007 to early 2009), 40%-45% of the world's wealth has been vaporized! This includes wealth across the entire spectrum, beginning with the working class, all the way to the world's richest multi-billionaires. Worth noting is that throughout the recent crash it has been just about impossible to find shelter from the ensuing deflationary storm now encircling all continents and zeroing in on all asset classes. <u>Asset protection</u> and <u>safeguarding one's wealth</u> in these times has been plagued by a virtual **lack of safety nets** anywhere; no hiding places and no sanctuaries (precious metals and US treasuries have to this point outperformed their peers, holding up better relative to other investments). Virtually not a single industry, nor the vast spectrum of commodities, nor most individual securities, mutual funds, real property etc. has been spared a direct hit. Global deflation and deleveraging is **on** and <u>raging</u>.

For the time being, the <u>secular deflationary story</u> and corresponding **vicious spiral of price deflation remains intact**: As America's citizens' (as well as those of other nations) wealth and prosperity (much of it built up over many generations) is quickly dissipating/melting away, world governments and economies have begun the process of imploding behind mounting towers of debt. With each passing day, escalating job losses are resulting in a further erosion of local, state, and federal tax revenues and helping to exacerbate ever-growing deficits. As to the genesis of real estate price deflation itself, due to the severity of our current credit/banking squeeze (banks have just about imposed a lending moratorium until or after housing prices stabilize), and lack of flow of credit (the lifeblood of all economies), housing prices are unable to find a bottom. A <u>downward vortex</u> has housing prices sinking as a result of job losses and foreclosures; job losses are mounting as a result of sinking real estate prices which are due in part to a correcting equity market, which in turn is leading to further corporate downsizing as a consequence of falling earnings.

Still following along? Loss of <u>consumer confidence</u> affects <u>consumer spending</u>. Loss of **consumer "wealth effect"** negatively affects consumer confidence. Falling revenues to local, state, and federal governments directly lead to layoffs, which again negatively affect the housing market and consumer confidence/consumer spending. **The catch-22:** All economic problems are in effect feeding off one another, fueling the downward cycle. As far as pinpointing the exact nature of the beast, or what came first -- the chicken or the egg -- suffice it to say for now, many factors are currently <u>feeding off one another,</u> helping to plummet much of the globe into the abyss.

Finally (insofar as the 21st Century Great Global Depression is concerned), **massive wealth destruction** and a change of spending patterns, atop other variables, is causing a seismic shift in people's lifestyles as well as <u>socio-economic status</u>: each tier, rung, or class of citizens from around the world is quickly <u>spiraling *down* the socio-economic ladder</u>.

Here's how this plays out: Some among the super rich are rapidly in danger of becoming the "generically rich," as yesterday's rich class is increasingly falling to a comfort level commensurate with (run of the mill) upper class citizens. The upper class, humbled as a result of recent events, now typifies the upper-middle class; the upper-middle class as a consequence is cascading downward to become the new <u>middle class</u>. What was once the middle class is rapidly deteriorating, getting immeasurably poorer -- as it stampedes down to a status of lower-middle class (or in instances where job losses are involved, all the way to the lower class). **Families suffering job losses in virtually all classes are losing their lifestyles at a disproportionately faster pace than their peers.** The lower class, trying desperately to keep its head above water, is now in the process of becoming indistinguishable from the poor; the poor today are catapulting downward to extreme poverty suffering disproportionately from a multitude of <u>negative</u> factors -- falling revenues to charities and lower levels of volunteerism, as well as prospective cutbacks in social services. Not your garden variety recession by any stretch of the imagination (as some in the media would like you to believe), this economic implosion is leaving folks high and dry, and down and out.

13

REAL ESTATE -- AND WHY IT <u>MUST</u> CONTINUE TO FALL
TRADITIONAL RESIDENTIAL REAL ESTATE VS. FORECLOSURES: A TALE OF TWO MARKETS
(**If you read no other part of my book, please read this chapter and weep along with me.**)

More shoes to drop…

Already (in a previous chapter) we've established the existence of a **vicious circle** whereby **falling home prices** serve as the <u>main catalyst</u> in perpetuating our current lending freeze, as banking institutions throughout the world get wet feet, afraid to make loans while the underlying security (in this instance the property itself) loses value. As a result of banks continuing their lending moratorium, real estate prices are negatively impacted due to fewer sales/closings, as well as due to deflation (lack of available credit in the economic engine) etc. Both <u>falling home prices</u> as well as a <u>restriction in lending</u> work in concert as one problem <u>accelerates</u> and <u>exacerbates</u> the other. This sinister combination of factors causes a downward vortex which leads to a further softening of the real estate market (and by extension a further tightening of bank lending).

Yet there is a more subtle but <u>far more sinister</u> trend

engulfing real estate today, driving prices downward. As someone who has been personally involved with real estate over the years -- buying, selling, renovating properties, working in the trenches...I've noted a foreboding pattern develop in the recent past which literally splits the real estate market (as we know it) in two. A closer look at today's residential real estate sales point to a schism in the market as **foreclosures** are increasingly becoming the <u>mainstay</u> for real estate sales; by contrast, the **non-foreclosure market** (relative to foreclosures) is <u>rapidly losing ground</u>. **Given that this trend is expected to continue unabated for some time to come, the foreclosure market is likely to grow into an even more prominent and dominant market.**

Specifically, a closer look tells us that foreclosures continue to take market share from overall sales (currently foreclosures account for a full ¼ of all real estate transactions). They are landing buyers as banks, brokers and other lenders, as well as local, state, and federal governments offer properties to the public at deep discounts. In contrast, the vast bulk of the traditional non-foreclosure residential real estate market -- much of it still out of touch with reality -- continues to hobble along with few buyers/bids, as sellers (in many instances) stubbornly hold on to the prospect that markets will somehow suddenly stabilize, reverse, and begin to bolt exponentially upward, just as in the past. Although of late seller denial has been mitigating somewhat, the fact remains that the <u>bulk</u> of today's traditionally priced inventory of homes listed for sale still fail the test of effectively competing in the open market. **The remedy: If home sellers are serious about getting bids on their properties -- now or in the near term -- they must <u>assimilate</u> to the healthy, "functional" market by drastically lowering asking prices to allow their properties to compete with today's foreclosures.** Stated in another way...the defunct "shadow" market of non-foreclosure traditionally priced homes (the bulk of homes offered for sale today) is under intense pressure to dramatically lower its prices in order to gain a competitive advantage in an environment of otherwise heavy foreclosure activity. (Escalating foreclosures are projected for years to come.) As such, THE OVERWHELMING MAJORITY OF HOMES LISTED FOR SALE TODAY ENCOMPASSING THE BETTER PART OF THE "TRADITIONAL" NON-FORECLOSURE INVENTORY ARE IN FACT **UN-SELLABLE** (at today's current asking prices).

In sum, given the economic backdrop of skyrocketing foreclosure rates projected for years to come (in just the next 12 months alone over two million residential foreclosures are expected to come to market), skyrocketing double-digit joblessness, an avalanche of homeowners simply walking away from "upside down" homes, millions of projected adjustable mortgage rate resets, etc., you have a recipe for a real estate maelstrom ready to put a major hurt on the American homeowner.

Summation and conclusion:

The US residential market has forked into two separate markets: a functional and growing foreclosure market and a dysfunctional "shadow market" of traditionally priced homes. The former market is currently driving sales (real estate closings) at deeply discounted rates as sellers from the larger, traditional (non-foreclosure) market are either forced to drastically reduce prices to compete with foreclosures or watch their properties languish on the market, often for years. AS A CONSEQUENCE OF TODAY'S ECONOMIC LANDSCAPE AND ESPECIALLY OUR BURGEONING FORECLOSURE MARKET, HOME PRICES ARE HEADED DOWNWARD. BARRING ADDITIONAL UNPRECEDENTED GOVERNMENTAL MEASURES, NOTHING IN THE WORLD CAN CURRENTLY STOP, REVERSE, OR IN ANY MAJOR WAY AMELIORATE REAL ESTATE'S OMINOUS DEFLATIONARY TREND.

Additional economic headwinds…

Commercial real estate has also recently begun an historic plunge which many believe will accelerate in 2010 and beyond. With retail industry bankruptcies continuing to climb and consumer spending still flatlining, with vacancy rates skyrocketing and rent values falling, commercial real estate is in a massive deflation. The potential ramifications of a collapse of this extremely large market (1.4 trillion dollars of outstanding loans are slated for refinancing within the next 18 months alone) will likely lead to a plethora of bank failures, further serve to restrict bank lending/flow of credit, and will likely lead to further economic weakness. The expected precipitous fall in the commercial real estate market/commercial lending weighs as a <u>chief factor</u> in the overall scheme of the Great Global Depression, reflecting a major component to our overall deflationary cycle.

Another time bomb for the real estate markets involves so-called <u>residential mortgage resets</u>. Mortgage "resets" are defined by a bumping up of interest rates on adjustable mortgages (often to dramatically higher rates), and typically lead to mass defaults by homeowners. Though we experienced a brief respite in 2009, 2010 and 2011 are <u>projected to be banner years for resets</u> (as well as for an escalation in commercial real estate loan refinancing). This phase, the "**Mother of All Resets**" is likely to be followed closely by an era known to most as the "<u>**Mother of all Mortgage Defaults**</u>." Ramifications of this "ground zero" Great Global Depression era event are likely to lead to a further obliteration of our overall economy and our real estate markets, as well as our equity markets, as it is likely to exacerbate the primary deflationary trend. **Woe to all homeowners (myself included) in getting through this critical phase.**

Finally, most will agree that over the past few years, banks engaged in a policy of collusion to keep defaulted properties from hitting the foreclosure market en masse due to their fear

of the effects on said markets. Banks, however, are increasingly coming under pressure to pull these properties out of limbo and dispense with them (this includes a vast inventory of REO properties (real estate owned properties). Other foreclosure "moratoriums," as well as stimulus imposed to give lenders and borrowers time to restructure their loans or to entice prospective buyers with tax credits, have either been terminated or are slated to end. Thus, as more bank-owned properties are brought to market (especially at heavily discounted prices), it is likely to cause an intensifying collapse in housing prices.

14

DARK CLOUDS ON THE HORIZON
EQUITIES MARKETS AND WHY THEY <u>WILL</u> <u>ULTIMATELY</u> CONTINUE TO CORRECT

A plethora of historical tell-tale evidence -- data, trends, and statistics -- converge to paint a grim picture of our economy and our equity markets moving forward. Ominous indicators tell us that recent selling is far from over, and that there are likely further legs of unwinding ahead for the current bear market cycle. History has a nasty habit of repeating itself; why the bottom is not in...

Let's start with a candid look at P/E (price/earnings) ratios. Based on historical mean averages, our current market valuations are out of whack. P/E ratios (or multiples, as they are known) are considered by far the best measure in valuing markets. (Markets are typically valued on the basis of twelve-month trailing earnings.) Our markets at present are telling the prudent investor, and for that matter anyone who will listen -- that our **global equity markets** sit atop a lofty perch. You might also refer to them as <u>divorced from reality</u> or describe them as (given our weak economic underpinnings) in <u>dangerous territory</u>! While market indexes such as the S&P 500 (The Standard & Poor's 500 index contains a basket of 500 of the most widely held stocks) have historically traded at P/E multiples of 15, today's broader markets averages and indexes currently trade at between 21-22 P/E (nearly a third above the historical average).

Indexes typically trend and trade above the historical norm during bull markets and below (in some instances well below) historical averages during **poor economic times** -- periods marked by deflation, recession, depression, stagflation, etc. -- which aptly describes our current circumstances. To bring the averages to within a more sustainable historical pricing, company earnings will need to accelerate in a major way, or the market will be left to settle the score and correct the imbalance. In fact, any sober and candid analysis of our equity markets (one which actually takes into account the overarching fundamentals of our economy) tells us that with the S&P 500 currently trading at a P/E multiple of over 20, alongside an overall economy which continues to weaken, with unemployment and foreclosures rising, with a specter of a double dip recession looming, there exists a burgeoning danger of a market blow-off (current market mania aside). The markets fully possess a <u>means</u> and a <u>motive</u> to dramatically correct (sell-off) from current levels.

I would not be surprised to see the markets find a bottom 60%-70% or more below today's levels (Dow 10,650), even if we never again see earnings fall off a cliff. If one were to factor in further economic contraction (a further precipitous drop in economic output), a market wipeout in line with the Great Depression…a 75%+ drop from current levels becomes plausible. Bear market bottoms typically bring P/E ratios down to 10 or lower (often to single digits), as market blow offs and climactic selling (typically associated with bear market bottoms) drive markets to their knees. Although the March 9th, 2009 lows brought climactic selling to be sure, the markets never dropped to even within a vicinity of their historic, bear market (mean) bottoms. Also of significance, **true** market bottoms are most often typified by a period in which the public spurns equities purchases, eventually leading to a complete <u>falling out of favor</u> for equities (something we also have yet to experience in this crisis). As such, March 2009's recent plunge did not achieve any of the significant historic bear market barometers, nor did it even begin to scratch the surface in terms of beginning to fully price in the depth and breadth of the economic contraction.

Conclusion:

The recent **rally** from March lows has served to further exacerbate the dislocation in the markets and place the markets in a more susceptible position to an extreme selloff. The grim reality of our current overheated/overpriced markets points to an eventual <u>reversion to the mean</u>, more ensuing market chaos, with deeper and more violent market corrections and/or crashes to come. Our equities markets (unless and until company earnings expeditiously and dramatically improve) are nearing the <u>precipice of a cliff</u>. In so saying, without a sharp reversal of current economic fortunes -- deteriorating economic fundamentals, rising unemployment, falling home prices, fallout from commercial real estate, falling consumer confidence, etc., selling pressure is likely to build, leading to an eventual market tumble.

The three "E's"...

More about how markets are valued and lessons gleaned from (what I term) the "Three E's": <u>Earnings, Equity Indexes, and Emotions</u>. As the stock market does not operate in a vacuum, it is important to point out that coexisting with the market is a host of factors which contribute to the daily bidding up and selling off of shares, and overall market values. While most of us recognize that the key driver of stock prices is **<u>earnings,</u>** earnings alone do not account for the pricing of a stock. The **<u>ebb and flow movement of the major indexes</u>** affects how individual issues (stocks, bonds, mutual funds, etc.) are priced; in essence one might consider individual equities "slaves" to the overall direction/macro movement of the stock market. (For example, on a typical trading day when the broader markets are showing nothing but red/down arrows indicating a market selloff, one would be hard-pressed to find an individual stock, ETF [exchange traded fund] or mutual fund with a green arrow pointed up.) Taking aside for a moment the first two E's -- earnings and overall equity market sentiment, the final E -- **emotions** or emotional factors (basic investor sentiment, fear, and greed) is typically responsible for further influencing the markets (and individual issues), driving market valuations to even greater extremes. If greed rules the day on Wall Street, bulls (out in force) are typically credited for catapulting the stock market upward. In contrast, when fear rules the day, even the strongest bulls may end up on the sidelines, scared out of the marketplace, or actively selling shares.

Further illustrating this point -- as to how emotions can wreak havoc with one's stock/bond/mutual fund portfolio, let's use the Standard & Poor's 500 index as an example: With the S&P trading at an historic mean of approximately 15 P/E -- purchase of a single share of the S&P would entail paying 15 times the price of the combined earnings for all 500 stocks in the S&P over the past 12 months (occasionally P/E ratios are used to reflect forward "projected" earnings). In higher, overheated, overextended markets, purchase of the very same share would likely cost the buyer a "premium" as he/she would be required to pay a multiple of 20-25 P/E or higher to own the same share. Finally, in contrast, during market bottoms this very same share of the S&P 500 index could typically be obtained at a "discount," or perhaps a "deep discount" relative to historical averages, with buyers having to dole out a P/E multiple as little as 5-8 for ownership of the S&P 500.

(Back to the first "E" -- earnings...)
It is critical that we take a moment to understand how markets are priced and why the potential for extreme volatility exists at any given moment: As previously noted, the market wages a constant battle within itself as it attempts to set the most *reliable* and *current* price/valuation based on investor sentiment as well as from a plethora of other factors. However, constantly shifting earnings

outlooks and earnings reports subject the price of individual stocks and/or securities to additional adjustments and fluctuations. For example, if the price for a particular stock or stock market index is otherwise stable, yet earnings disappoint, the current market price (a direct byproduct of price and earnings) can instantly appear more expensive (from one day to the next, even from one minute to the next). Conversely, if the price for a particular stock or stock market index is stable, yet earnings surprise to the upside, a stock, index or other security can instantly become "inexpensive" -- having the appearance as though it just went "on sale." **In sum:** Even slight changes in earnings expectations often lead to gyrating P/E ratios, and by extension, ever-shifting valuations in the underlying security(s).

Our real estate conundrum:

As previously noted, a continuation of the unresolved problem of an <u>incipient decline in real estate</u> is likely to weigh on overall equity markets and inspire additional rounds of <u>deleveraging,</u> causing further selloffs in global equities markets. Here's how a falling real estate market impacts global equity indexes: A vicious circle (not the first one we've seen here) begins whereby falling real estate prices cause more delinquencies and personal bankruptcies, and ultimately more foreclosures. Foreclosures serve to hurt banks and borrowers alike in a major way: bankrupting institutions, slamming consumers, and wiping out lending, which ultimately fuels deflationary flames and leads to a further depressing of real estate prices. Bank balance sheets (banks continue to remain highly leveraged by every historical measure) are in turn annihilated by falling real estate prices which further leads to cataclysmic sell-offs, as institutions scramble to meet margin requirements, etc. The more leveraged an institution, the faster it falls in a down market, with big money players scrambling to raise capital as market panic and additional rounds of deleveraging play out. Deleveraging *comes in like* *a lamb but can quickly leave like a lion* as it asserts and reinforces itself -- engulfing whole all those who stand in its way. Selling begets selling as routine market corrections build steam, potentially leading to market crashes. Conclusion: Falling US real estate prices put pressure on US equities markets, which in turn cause most global markets to sell off in tandem. The problem as I see it is that stabilization of the US and global real estate markets are still a ways off.

Dow/Gold Ratio as prognosticator:

A select group of some of the most keen and savvy economists, investors, market observers, and perma-bears swear by the Dow/Gold Ratio as a highly valid tool in predicting future market performance. This prognosticator establishes a recurring trend over the past century (at 35-45 year intervals), whereby a combination of a falling Dow Jones Industrial Average and soaring gold and commodities markets cause the Dow (specifically a share of the Dow Jones Industrial Average) to sell on par with or roughly on par with an ounce of gold. While in 1999 we saw the spread between the Dow and gold widen to over 40 times with the Dow trading at a mighty $11,000+ to gold's pitiful $250-$300 per ounce, today the spread/gap has been steadily closing. In fact the past ten years or so have served to close the Dow/Gold gap to approximately nine (at recent count). My personal view, and if history is any guide, is that we will likely see a further narrowing of the spread, eventually leading to an on par or near congruous relationship between Dow and gold, with both trading at between $2,500-$3,500.

Not as outlandish a proposition as you might think...to get there all that would be required is a further 2/3 correction of the Dow from current valuations in combination with a doubling to tripling of today's gold prices. (I remind the reader that in recent years we've already witnessed the Dow plunge roughly in half as we've witnessed gold prices more than quadruple from their lows.) The gap is narrowing; the relationship grows tighter -- just like a tide moving in and out on a warm summer's night, a magical, mystical, magnetic plane continues to pull the two historic polar opposites closer together…

Wall Street thrives while Main Street dives…

While this temporary divergence exists today, it will not in the long run, for the two are intrinsically tied together. Eventually an overall weakening economy replete with escalating foreclosures, personal and corporate bankruptcies, escalating unemployment, and falling consumer confidence and spending will directly (and with a vengeance) *impact company earnings,* leading to further market corrections. With the "Two Streets" enjoying a symbiotic relationship, the notion of a "jobless recovery" (a phrase heard often in the news) is a misnomer, quite frankly **hogwash.** Keep in mind the US government, compliments of the Fed and the Treasury, have already fired off virtually all of their various economic weapons/ammunition -- reducing rates to near 0%, incipiently printing trillions of dollars, presenting America with various stimulus and/or spending packages, bailing out companies and industries in trouble…throwing in everything but the "kitchen sink" to instigate inflationary (anti-deflationary) pressures in the economy -- and as yet has been unable to instigate a vibrant or sustainable recovery. **Jobs still remain scarce, consumer spending is anemic, real estate continues to fall, and a sustainable earnings recovery remains questionable at best**. In the long run, the relationship between Wall Street and Main Street can be summed up with the following slogan: **As Main Street dives, Wall Street is KO'd!**

CAUTION SIGN on the TRACK; conclusion and summation:

The dislocation in the markets will not go on indefinitely; something will give sooner or later. The markets will demand higher earnings or they will **instigate sharp selloffs** to forcibly lower PE multiples. (Mind you, Standard & Poor's projects earnings to remain feeble for at least the balance of 2010 and 2011.) Any number of catalysts have the potential to bring about a so-called <u>key reversal day</u>, a day signaling and signifying an interim market top, and lead to the commencement of a market plunge to new depths. As fear once again begins to reassert itself on the markets, selling pressure will build bringing the broader averages -- the Dow, the S&P, the Nasdaq market, etc. either more in line (or likely below) their historical (mean) valuations. In so saying, a further drop from current market levels of between 65%-70% or more is not only plausible, but likely.

Regardless, the next few years are likely to be critical in terms of helping to define our economy for the next generation. If our current deep recession turns into a full-blown depression as I believe it will, if the secular bear lurches forward mauling everything in its path as I fear he may, it is not out of the realm of possibility to see the Dow trading at 1991-1993 levels.

Finally, let us not forget the ominous historic precedent which states that <u>BUBBLES NEVER POP HALFWAY</u>. Just recognizing this one fact should serve to keep the reader (and hopefully the prospective investor) on his/her toes.

15

DEBT-RIDDEN CITIZENS ON THE BRINK
HIGHER TAX RATES ARE ON THE WAY AND HERE TO STAY, PLUS OTHER UNINTENDED CONSEQUENCES OF MASSIVE GOVERNMENT SPENDING

Somebody has to pay for it…why not you and me?

 The US federal budget continues to <u>hemorrhage money</u> due to the effects of a severely contracting economy, as exemplified by the ominous combination of a shrinking tax base and massive government spending (many local and state governments are faring no better, for that matter). As the national debt clock continues to run out of available zeros and commas, Uncle Sam grows fiscally weaker by the day, hour, even minute -- leaving Americans more indebted and America one step closer to <u>insolvency</u>. Our imploding economy continues to flatline in spite of massive government efforts to provide the necessary spark to breathe new life into the patient. The government needs money and it needs it yesterday. So what's it to do?

Let's recap:

 Government, in addition to fighting two wars on two fronts plus a global War on Terror, is waging a full-out battle against global deflation, a war to stem the tide of joblessness, as well as a fight to unfreeze credit markets. The military is stretched and battle-fatigued, with some soldiers currently serving three and/or four tours of duty in both Iraq and Afghanistan. Our printing presses (already operating at an historically torrid pace) threaten to cause a global shortage of paper and ink (I digress), as unintended consequences of our policies are paving the way for an eventual trouncing in the value of US currency, all the while fueling a risk of future inflation and/or hyperinflation. Our banking system, the very essence of capitalism, is in tatters and on life support, requiring massive doses of financial support, bailouts, and other "stimulus" just to survive. State and local governments are spiraling downward due to a severe falloff in income and real estate tax revenue, with many operating in complete shambles, stretched to their limits...in some instances becoming totally overwhelmed and paralyzed by **massive budgetary deficits**. It's time for government to pull out all the stops... which unfortunately for many on Capitol Hill today means raising capital from the **true lender of last resort** -- the American taxpayer. As such, it is inevitable that sooner or later the government will have no choice but to effectively, <u>declare war on its own citizenry</u> to fund current budget deficits and massive government spending.

Uncle Sam's principal methods for generating, creating, and/or increasing revenue are as follows (Mind you, as Uncle Sam fights to keep the global economy in a semblance of working order please note the following statistic -- according to a recent article posted on MSNBC.com, the current drop off in federal tax revenues is so catastrophic that it represents the greatest falloff in federal revenues since 1932 -- since during the very heart and height of the Great Depression.)

First and foremost (historically the least invasive method), Uncle Sam holds auctions whereby **US treasuries (US debt) is packaged and sold to investors** (domestic and foreign). While at present, this still represents a semi-viable option (ironically, interest in US treasuries still remains high due to US Federal Reserve bond market purchases as well as by virtue of the fact that some investors consider them a safe harbor for parking one's moneys during times of volatility), foreigners in particular have begun to shun treasuries and by extension, the US dollar and dollar denominated assets. Thus, foreign purchase of US treasury debt has slowed of late. (The world has had ample opportunity to consider, analyze, and scrutinize the US's current economic policies -- especially as they relate to our massive government bailouts, spending, and interventions -- and has correctly concluded that our policies are highly destructive to US paper, specifically the US dollar and US bonds.) Others are avoiding the US bond market, recognizing that short term rates of near $0.00 are wholly unsustainable and that an outright **violent purge** of the US treasury market may be in the offing. Unthinkable just a few years back, Uncle Sam as Mecca (and powerhouse) for safeguarding one's money is increasingly coming under scrutiny as worries abound regarding America's future. Confidence in American investments has also been shaken as a result of recent market turmoil. US treasuries, historically considered among the safest havens and a virtually sacrosanct investment, are now seen increasingly as a poor, even unsound <u>long-term investment</u> by many today.

Second, can you say "boy knows how to hustle"? Uncle Sam plays the role of **"sugar daddy"** and cranks the printing presses 'round the clock (24/7), flooding the global markets with "cheap" dollars in an all-out effort to stimulate economic growth. At its beck and call, the US Treasury incessantly continues to work overtime, printing massive quantities of freshly minted US greenback as a <u>front line defense</u> against **economic collapse** and for use as the weapon of choice against a general **war on deflation**. This policy at present maintains majority support in Congress as aiding ailing companies, industries, and banks deemed "too big to fail" is seen as the best way forward under the present set of circumstances. That said, today many politicians in Washington as well as business leaders are beginning to ask questions about the <u>end game</u>, wondering what unforeseen consequences lie ahead, not the least of which is a future drag on the economy. Excessive spending by the Fed and Treasury is increasingly seen for what it is…an inflation threat and <u>unsustainable policy</u>. Controlling US federal spending and reducing US budget deficits is something the world is now beginning to demand as well. Thus sooner than later, and for a wide variety of reasons, unrestrained printing of US greenbacks will grind to a halt.

Last but not least…(the final leg of the troika for US federal revenue creation):

The third method (surely the least popular) for generating revenue (used by state and local governments as well) **involves ratcheting up tax rates.** Governments, large and small, will always find <u>reasons</u> and a <u>rationale</u> to justify their need for additional revenue, as citizens will typically retain their right to be duly displeased when the tax man comes a-knocking. In so saying, Uncle Sam will use the argument that more money is needed to fund current and future bailouts; he will claim that more moneys are needed to fight global deflation, the massive retrenchment and contraction in credit and consumerism, and to compensate for falling tax revenues. He will tell us that more capital injections are needed to fund an aging baby boom population requiring Social Security, Medicare, and Medicaid; as well as government pensions; the new healthcare initiative, etc. He will give these reasons and many others for raising your and my taxes (none of which include cutting spending).

Raising of tax rates in today's economic climate is igniting a rebellion from taxpayers as the **timing of the rate hikes could not be worse.** The average citizen, although being up to his/her eyeballs in debt is presently working to reduce his/her overall debt load and has even begun saving again -- at recent count, up to 5% of his/her moneys. The "Average Joe" is also busy licking his wounds from a historic mauling by the market bear, suffering injuries to his overall personal wealth, investment portfolio, home value, and job security, and is often a stone's throw away from foreclosure, or in some instances has already been laid off from his job. Thus, he has no patience for hearing about his government's pain or needs (which are numerous), whatever the reason. Americans are already stretched far too thin and thus many are revolted at even the thought of trying to keep up with the growing and vigorous demands of the federal, state, and local taxman. A showdown is surely in the offing.

"Average Joe" finds allies...

With tax protests on the rise and some predicting full-blown tax revolts not far behind, it is essential to understand the source of "Tea Party" anger, to delve into the belly of the beast as it were: In a nutshell, the TEA PARTY MOVEMENT is (by and large) a middle-class revolt. The middle class, representing the majority of American taxpayers, has become increasingly discontent with government, feeling disenfranchised and disillusioned with government, in disagreement with government's "too big to fail" policy of bailouts and spending habits, the running up of budget deficits, etc. and has taken to (blow horn in hand) hammering away at such themes as need to end the nanny state, quest for smaller government, the mantra of you can't get blood from a stone etc. Many middle of the road Americans are livid about out of control federal spending and the prospects for higher taxes (most acknowledge that our economic problems are a complex issue that has taken many years to develop and that no one **magic bullet** exists for solving America's burgeoning financial problems). Tea Party supporters and other middle class Americans believe that they are the ones who have been disproportionately affected by the Great Recession, in addition to being incessantly "squeezed" by the taxman, and are as a result the ones left holding the short end of the stick. Furthermore, they are convinced (and with good evidence to boot) that citizens in their ranks are disproportionately falling through the cracks...and now they've had enough!

◄ 21ST CENTURY GREAT GLOBAL DEPRESSION

Between a rock and a hard place; the battle lines have been drawn

On one hand, those opposed to the Tea Party movement argue that raising taxes (at least on some Americans) is an essential component to bringing us out of our current economic quagmire, believing that our tax rates have been too low for far too long, and that larger government is the answer to most or all of our problems. On the other hand, Tea Party-ers and other fiscal conservatives believe that cutting and controlling spending, not raising taxes, is the way to go. At present, discontent continues to escalate among America's electorate toward Washington's current fiscal posture and as a result, a challenge is being mounted to current administration policy. Which ideology prevails in the end no one knows with certainty -- though in the meantime, rest assured, a collision course is set between the two factions -- THE TAXMAN (and by extension those supporting bigger government), and TAXPAYERS (led by members of the Tea Party Movement).

A few words regarding the recent passage of the health care bill…

Let me stipulate that America can and ought to do better to improve the lives of 37 million American citizens who suffer without medical coverage (roughly 1 in 9 Americans has no health care insurance), yet none of us has the privilege to live in a vacuum. IF WE DON'T PUT OUR ECONOMY ON A SUSTAINABLE FISCAL FOOTING, WE WILL END UP PUTTING 9 OUT OF 9 (100%) OF AMERICANS AT **GRAVE** RISK (including today's uninsured). Rebuilding our economy from ground up first, improving critical safeguards to homeland security, balancing our budgets, fixing a crippled global financial system, and gaining energy independence **must come first**. Continue to get in over our heads now, go for broke, and we risk all as well as accelerate our demise. No one ever said maintaining the American Empire would not be an <u>expensive proposition.</u> All the same, radically overhauling our broken health care system cannot be accomplished in an era of multi-trillion-dollar deficits. **We can't have our cake and eat it too.**

Solutions...

Finally, if the American dream is to endure, Congress will need to pass a Balanced Budget Amendment, as government will be required to adopt a **pay as we go** philosophy. We'll need to wrestle control of our budgets and re-evaluate our commitments home and abroad -- in the end maintaining the most essential programs, cutting excess spending wherever possible, and funding our most critical programs -- without massive money printing or accounting gimmicks. Government will need to begin to shoot straight. Anyone reading between the lines of a government CBO [Congressional Budget Office] report is likely to find the reporting overly optimistic, the projections largely inaccurate or useless...sometimes even laughable. (Keep in mind Social Security costs today are a full 900% above original CBO projections.) We will need to impose <u>strict oversight</u> over all government-sponsored social programs, <u>requiring</u> them to remain solvent. While no one wants to be the bearer of bad tidings (Republicans or Democrats), leveling with the public as to the dire state of our entitlement programs, and telling us what cutbacks will be necessary in the future, go in hand with getting our fiscal house in order. We either learn to live within our means and within budgets or we <u>forfeit our collective future as a nation</u>. It's really that simple.

P.S. They say that in life **there are few absolutes.** Well here's one: **Budget deficits cannot be maintained indefinitely!**

16

IT'S STILL NOT TOO LATE TO THINK AND ACT AS A <u>CONTRARIAN</u>
(BESIDES, YOU'RE IN GOOD COMPANY. CHRIST WAS ONE TOO.)

It's war in the ring…let's get ready to rumble: bulls, bears, contrarians, as well as the general masses "status-quo-tarians" battle for turf…

Due to the <u>extreme nature of today's volatile markets</u>, I must remind the reader that the **first rule of thumb** and **priority** for today's investor should start with a candid review of his/her investment portfolio, a thorough assessment of risk, and a focus on <u>capital preservation</u>. Parking one's money in the market while expecting it to grow year over year (typical of secular bull markets) does not apply during these treacherous times. **<u>Trading</u>** equities, as a rule (as opposed to investing) falls short as well; Just as "flipping homes" attempts to capitalize on market momentum, trading equities, a strategy defined by **moving in and out of** stocks, mutual funds as well as bonds, currencies, commodities, futures, options etc., carries with it the potential for mind boggling profits or <u>losses</u>…typically the latter. (Furthermore, trading stocks requires an appetite for risk far above most investors' appetites.) Finally, an investment strategy based on putting all of one's eggs in one basket/betting on a single

IT'S STILL NOT TOO LATE TO THINK...

market outcome – be it an inflationary one or a deflationary one, or perhaps betting solely on a new longterm US bull market -- does not represent a *diversified* investment plan.

That said, this leaves the vast majority of today's investors faced with a plethora of tough choices -- whether to stay true to one's investment philosophy and/or strategy, or give in to the media hype, thereby allowing oneself to be coerced into various new investment schemes, trading platforms, and/or investment vehicles. Today's investor finds him/herself in a tug of war -- being pulled in numerous directions at the same time -- offered every financial pitch under the sun. He or she is forced to battle information overload -- barraged by a constant stream of 24/7 financial market coverage, financial market advice and "propaganda," market predictions and prognostication, as well as endless recommendations and hype. Add to this investor propensity for displaying extremes in market sentiment (fear and greed) as exhibited by recent **panic selling** (and of late, **panic buying),** and the stage is set for full-blown investor neurosis.

Separating the wheat from the chaff and fact from fiction is essential to one's ability to maintain a successful investment posture/ healthy financial portfolio. *How do we propose to embark on a journey of successful investing, sidestepping the land mines (financial kisses of death), filtering out successful stock recommendations and sound market advice from the plethora of mass-media noise, hot stock tips, and unending streams of poor financial advice? Whom can we trust or look to for guidance in these treacherous economic times? What lessons can be gleaned from recent market performance?*

While there is no simple answer to these questions, one thing is certain -- as a betting man, I would advise to take the bet **against** the vast majority of popular culture financial advice and hype in favor of crafting and fine-tuning one's own investment strategy, preferably with the help of a few select, capable, and trusted financial planners. Mainstream (popular culture) financial gurus, though correct in their predictions from time to time, are more often than not flat-out wrong in their predictions, totally off-base with their market analysis and recommendations -- often priming and pumping the public with completely erroneous information. There are surely a few out there that are (as Warren Buffet puts it) "wired for this game," but make no mistake -- they are far and few between.

Drawing the battle lines...

In the near corner, weighing in at 90%-95% of the population, I present to you the reigning champions, the **"status-quo-tarians,"** as I refer to them. Most everyone in this camp (a typical cross-section of society) -- Wall Street bankers, brokers and other financial "experts," political pundits and commentators, economists, policy makers, senators, politicians of all stripes, butchers, shopkeepers, dentists, lawyers, administrators, UPS deliverymen, retired folk, bricklayers, lumberjacks, pastry chefs, Republicans, Democrats, ideologues, Federal Reserve chairmen as well as a US president or five -- make up this diverse group that in most instances has been programmed for a lifetime to believe in the mantra of betting "long" (**buying** securities, specifically US equities); never "shorting" stocks, bonds, etc. (Shorting a stock involves borrowing a particular issue, and selling it with the expectation that the stock price is likely to fall.) Brainwashed by a steady diet of blind optimism they believe that it is their **birthright** or **implicit patriotic duty** to continue to prop up markets, especially our own, often to their personal detriment. Many in this group (some to this very day) have been conditioned to believe that "buying dips" is part and parcel of a winning strategy. Others (against all rhyme and reason) continue to employ the "buy and hold" strategy of buying stocks and other equities and holding on to them for the long haul even as this method has been fairly discredited over the past decade or so. All share the common belief that **in the long run stocks are the best place to be.** (Not to get too philosophical or cynical...but who of us knows which of us will even be blessed with long life, experience a "long run" ourselves so as to have the opportunity to ride out the eddies

IT'S STILL NOT TOO LATE TO THINK... ►

and currents in the market?)

So entrenched are the status-quo-tarians -- if you were to try bringing up the topic and prospects of global deflation to this crowd, they are likely to stare at you with a blank expression as if they were a zombie. Financial analysts from this warm and fuzzy crowd who feed the public a steady diet of buy recommendations...the "Goldilocks" flock if you will (among them many in the media with bully pulpit and bullhorn -- great cheerleaders of optimism) have in many instances helped lead entire swaths of humanity down the road to financial ruin. Yet they are given a pass by most, for they share the same investing ideology with the majority of the public. *Who in this group warned of the coming dangers for the markets ahead? Which of them predicted the breadth and scope of Wall Street's collapse and imminent market turmoil? How many called a market top or recommended their clients proceed with caution in late 2007? Given the cataclysmic events in the markets of late and with a poor track record to boot, shouldn't most status-quo-tarians think twice before parking their hard earned moneys with like-minded brokers and financial planners?* **What ever happened to once bitten, twice shy???**

In the far corner, weighing in at perhaps 5%-10% of the population, swimming against the tide of popular opinion and investor sentiment are the **contrarians** (and in some instances, the "perma-bears"). Unwavering in their position -- telling it like it is, marching to the beat of their own drums, possessing great degrees of "chutzpah"...these lonely and often ridiculed souls, although smaller in numbers, have been gathering strength of late. Some have made vast, powerful, accurate, and prescient predictions on the markets, warning investors to either raise cash allocations in their portfolios or in some instances short the market outright (place bets against the market and/or individual issues with the expectation that markets are headed lower). Often vilified by the entrenched news media and financial establishment, this often awkward and less-than-synchronized group has (in my opinion) approached the market using a more appropriate wider lens -- attempting to predict what's in store for the markets in context of the macro-global economy, as compared to simply focusing on the next earnings report. Many in this crowd have continued relentlessly to warn the public of the deep, underlying fiscal problems in our overall economy, their words often falling on deaf ears. I'm hoping it won't take the Dow imploding to 3,500 for the "doom and gloom" crowd to gain visibility among the general public...for the masses to recognize that contrarians represent a <u>legitimate voice</u> (a voice of reason, I argue) <u>in the greater scheme of investing</u>, but as a good contrarian myself, I understand that public sentiment is not likely to turn until just such a time.

Proof that "status-quo-tarians" are not infallable...

Many of the world's most legendary and successful businessmen and investors have been especially hard hit, even brutalized by the recent market selloff: Warren Buffet's Berkshire Hathaway got its clock cleaned just like most other companies, to the tune of nearly 50% (25 billion dollars of wealth destruction in 2008 for guru Warren Buffet alone). Bill Gates' wealth (adjusted for inflation) is down over 70% in the past decade or so. CNBC's Jim Cramer -- the man who consistently advises his listeners to "stay in the game"-- fared no better than anyone else as the equity in his charitable trust was sliced nearly in half during the equity market crash of 2007-2009. Famed Saudi prince Alwaleed purchased billions of dollars in Citibank shares at approximately $30.00 only to watch his shares plummet down below $1.00 before rebounding. Many of our top real estate moguls are being especially hard hit by the impact and depth of the ongoing real estate correction -- very few having taken the pre-emptive steps to reduce market exposure and/or downsize their companies ahead of the fray. In sum, the crowd of the world's richest -- **billionaires all** -- including a host of Indian, Chinese, and Russian tycoons, cumulatively lost a combined equity of 1.5 trillion dollars during recent market turmoil.

IT'S STILL NOT TOO LATE TO THINK...

In the end, no matter whom you speak to, you are likely to get a different opinion and analysis on the markets. Some folks are adamant as to their belief that we have just entered a **new bull market.** Others will swear we are in a **bear market rally/bull market trap** (the latter so says this humble author). No matter, all of us should agree that *true economic growth* and prosperity can be obtained only on a solid economic foundation and footing -- one not clouded by an insolvent banking system replete with dubious accounting methods, treasury policies aimed at the destruction of the dollar, exponentially exploding debt loads, rising unemployment (just over a year ago we were losing 20,000+ jobs per day), a tide of personal and corporate bankruptcies, steadily falling and deflating real estate prices, global contraction of credit, global deleveraging, and so on. The case for a new bull market becomes even more suspect when one factors in the following ominous current trends: growing federal, state, and local budget deficits due to imploding tax revenues, exploding federal debt obligations to Social Security, Medicare, Medicaid, etc., and the rapid aging of our baby boom generation.

Conclusion:

Chalk one up for the contrarians, the fringe players, even the perma-bears; arguably this time, they've hit the nail on the head. Swimming against the tide of popular opinion may not be such a bad thing after all; one day it may even save your financial life.

Fellow investor…think you've had enough? If you're ready to face your greatest investment fears, if you want to think and act independent of the herd, if you're ready to think and act boldly…to lead rather than follow; ready to shed investment strategies based on hope…come aboard, fellow contrarian. **Welcome aboard!**

17

UNCHARTED WATERS
BAILOUT NATION AND RELENTLESS MONEY PRINTING BY THE US TREASURY

Ben Bernanke and the Federal Reserve attempt to "trade up" deflation for inflation, plus going mad...politicians with bailout fever...

    The <u>**high stakes game**</u> of extensive money printing to stimulate the economy does not come without its own mountain of risk. For starters, there are no guarantees that current US Fed and Treasury policies will ultimately prevail in curbing global deflation or lead to a sustained recovery of failed industries -- banking, automotive, and insurance (AIG). The US Treasury may end up pouring trillions of dollars in taxpayer moneys, propping up defunct companies and industries, only to watch them fail in the end. Other unintended consequences of massive money printing includes the potential trading off of the destruction of one asset class (tangible goods, homes, cars, etc.) with another (most notably the US dollar, US treasuries, etc.). Apples and oranges, you say? Not as far as I'm concerned.

    Case in point: In a perfect world, <u>a modest dose of stimulus and inflation</u> would be sufficient to stabilize the real estate market and/or inspire confidence back to consumers, and ultimately translate into reviving the broader economy. However, to this point, more than a

UNCHARTED WATERS

dozen trillion dollars of current and future federal stimulus have not produced a strong recovery, nor created healthy job growth, nor has it breathed new life into our ailing retail market. If our all-out efforts to stabilize the global economy come up short, we will (as a result of massive spending) be left in a far worse fiscal state in which to deal with the ramifications of the economic meltdown. As such, <u>risks in choosing the proper course of action have never been higher</u>.

Do you recall Indiana Jones's predicament at the end of the movie "Search for the Holy Grail" when he is admonished by the knight to **choose wisely**? Let us all <u>hope</u> and <u>pray</u> that Ben Bernanke, Chairman of the Fed and Timothy Geithner, head of Treasury have indeed chosen wisely. Consequences of choosing the wrong path in reviving our economy are likely to be **catastrophic**.

The Fed's goal of stopping deflation and/or creating low inflation is easier said than done: The proposition that the Fed can actually inflate our economy to a predetermined point, then cap inflation at this very same point, is pure fiction. Popular culture theories have us believing instead that once the "inflation genie" has been released, she is hard to put back into the bottle. The notion that the US Fed in concert with other global Federal Reserve banks can create inflation, flooding markets with endless trillions of dollars, euros, and yen and still retain the ability to manipulate the (target) inflation rate to a desired 2%-3% is <u>what fairy tales are made of</u>. The reality is that the Fed is likely to overshoot and do so in a big way. Coincidentally, if anyone you knew handled their personal financial obligations (as has our government in the recent past) in a way that caused them to double their balance sheet (deficits) over the course of a year or two, showing only measurable improvement in bottom line revenue/income, they would likely be considered on a <u>fast track to insolvency and bankruptcy.</u>

On a contrasting note, some suggest that the Fed's policies to inflate are <u>not without rhyme or reason</u> since a devalued US currency serves to alleviate a percentage of our debt burden, as money becomes in-effect less "equitable," and our debts

less "valuable." While this may indeed be true, it does not come without a host of *drawbacks*. Our weakening currency serves to diminish our bargaining power and clout with respect to our creditors, most notably China, Japan, India, Brazil, Russia, and other nations holding the majority of US treasury debt. Other drawbacks and/or unintended consequences of said policies include potential for gross devaluation of US currency, loss of confidence in US dollar as global reserve currency, mortgaging of future economic growth by stifling our economy with higher interest rates, risk of overinflating our economy, risk of hyperinflation, the burdening of future generations with inescapable debt, and so on. Inflating away our currency in an attempt to diminish our debt load is a complex matter with a plethora of unintended consequences!

Have we chosen wisely?

As I've intimated in the forward, it takes a great deal of audacity and chutzpah to run up a massive tab and a suffocating debt load as our government is currently in the process of doing today, and expect our children and our grandchildren to "flip for it." That said, we are after all a **representative democracy** and the will of the people passes along to our representatives (moving up the chain of command, as it were), taking the form of the will of the politicians! As such, the ball is now in *their* court and politicians in Washington are indicating a further fervent desire to **print and spend.** *How long will their efforts last?* On the horizon lurks a growing challenge to this ideology. Stay tuned to the upcoming November elections to see how this plays out.

In the meantime, how will history record our actions today? *Will the consensus of historians believe we had gotten it right? Noble intentions aside, will our current spending binge be considered justifiable under the present set of circumstances? Furthermore, how will we be remembered by posterity? Will those of us living today be remembered as a pathetic bunch trying to make the best out of* *a dismal situation, or as blatantly un-American in spirit...weasels lacking sufficient honor, integrity, and fortitude to bite the proverbial bullet and pay for our own economic misdeeds?*

Hyperinflation must be avoided at all costs...

Although one may debate the merits of whether inflation or deflation is a bigger threat to our overall economy and economic well-being, we can all agree that hyperinflation is the *ultimate economic game changer*. As deflation wreaks havoc on most asset classes, and inflation causes prices to rise and profits to fall, it is **hyperinflation** which carries the potential to drastically lower living standards for all by crushing the nation's currency, in effect, thrusting a nation back into the stone age.

Thus, my view of current Fed policy is analogous to a fire crew attempting to fight an isolated forest fire by dropping a MOAB bomb (mother of all bombs). Instead of just putting out the fire using traditional methods, the fire crew uses **overkill** to put out the fire, and the ensuing explosion -- while sucking out all the air in the area -- vaporizes and incinerates everything in its path. Although the fire crew is successful in putting out the initial fire, the collateral damage has been overwhelming. The entire forest has been burned to the ground.

Conclusion:

There are more measured and less volatile ways to fight price deflation than by our current high-stakes policy of endless money printing and bailouts. Furthermore, it is possible to view deflation as part and parcel of a necessary and healthy recalibration of prices, just as forest fires are often known to add to the overall health of the ecosystem.

18

ENTER THE 20,000 POUND GORILLA
NEGATIVE ECONOMIC IMPACT FROM AN AGING BABY BOOM GENERATION

Effects from our largest and soon to be retiring baby boom generation are likely to be widespread and have a devastating effect on our G.D.P for years to come. As this aging generation (72 million strong) shifts from income producers to requiring federal, state, and local subsidies, the consequences are likely to induce gaping holes in revenue from sea to shining sea...

    This metamorphosis (whose effects will begin to be felt in 2010 and stretch for well more than a decade), will serve to exacerbate an already severely hobbled economy, and is likely to lead to (according to my calculations) a net loss of between 10-12 million jobs as well as a rise in the base unemployment rate of between 6%-8%. <u>Funny how no one seems to be talking about this!</u>
    Beginning 2010, as the oldest baby boomers turn 65, we can expect an average net loss of more than ¾ million jobs from payrolls each year, with this trend raging on for nearly a decade and a half. (Don't expect employers to rush to fill these positions -- if ever -- given current economic conditions.) <u>All of this is projected to occur at a time when revenues will be in desperate need of growing and expanding</u> (current federal, state, and local revenues

are squarely in retrograde).

With unemployment already hovering at just under 10% (most economists concede that even if we began a robust recovery starting today, unemployment is likely to spike to at least 11% or 12%) the economic impact from our retiring baby boom generation alone has the potential to raise our unemployment rate by 50% or more from current levels. As if more bad news was needed…Americans, already in **thrift mode,** will likely increasingly embrace a universal "miser" or "tightwad" mindset as baby boomers rein in spending in their twilight years. The aging of the baby boom generation (as well as the rapid aging of other mature like-minded economies in the world today) represents one of the top five factors/catalysts in my assertion that we are facing a 2/3 wipeout of world commerce over the next 15-20 years.

The worst is yet to come…

The worst is far from over; the effects from a retiring baby boom generation have not even begun to register on the radar… on our economy or our overall markets. While the markets have begun the process of discounting certain aspects of a sinking global economy -- the credit crisis, a residential housing collapse, a falloff in company earnings, and to some degree rising unemployment, the markets have not begun to factor in a host of other problems, to wit: an impending correction/crash of the US bond market, a substantially higher interest rate environment, the "jobless" recovery, further unwinding in commercial real estate, additional rounds of global deflation and deleveraging, the extreme indebtedness and near-insolvency of the US government especially as it pertains to unfunded liabilities (70 or more trillion dollars at last count), further deleveraging and/or collapse in the derivatives markets, overly optimistic pricing of today's stock market with regard to historically high P/E multiples, projected double-digit unemployment rates for years on end, a potential collapse of the US greenback/world reserve currency, a looming specter of soaring oil and/or commodity prices, as well as the deleterious effects on our economy from a retiring baby boom generation. As you have surmised by now, markets often do not present themselves as shining examples of <u>rationality</u>, <u>logic</u>, or <u>efficiency</u>, but one thing is certain…sooner or later, there always comes a **day of reckoning.**

19

WOE TO GENERATION "Y"
PRAY FOR OUR <u>LOST</u> GENERATION

Born to such promise, Generation Y (b. 1983-2000) also known as "Millennials," represent our first truly tech-savvy generation as they have been born and bred, taught, and reared in the age of computers, the worldwide web, and email, as well as the era of cell phones, text messaging, etc. They were destined to make their predecessors look bad.

Typically smart and communal in their approach, they are known to be far more health-oriented and in some instances more mature, rational-thinking and rational-acting than their predecessors. Sophisticated, ambitious, instinctively knowing right from wrong (more often than not), they were to <u>take the world by storm</u>! After all, how could the previous "clunkier," more dated, technologically less sophisticated generations compete pound for pound in an ever-swift, ever-changing, information age?

Instead as it turns out, (defying logic) the pendulum has swung 180 degrees in the opposite direction -- fast and furiously. The broken global economy has made a mockery out of Generation Y-ers' leverage in the workplace, turning it quickly into a disadvantage. Youthfulness, pizzazz, likeability, charm and/or sophistication go only so far in a job market that continues to contract. Those with higher degrees being termed "<u>overqualified</u>" in our current market is a distinct disadvantage as well.

How far the tables have turned…X-ers (born 1965-1982) and

baby boomers (born 1946-1964)…even pre-baby boomers are enjoying a whole series of distinct advantages over Gen Y-ers. For starters, most have prospered as a result of having lived a portion of or most of their lives in what I term the <u>Grand Era of Credit Expansion</u>. This has allowed previous generations the ability and opportunity to amply establish themselves. Many have further used **easy credit** to grow and promote their <u>own</u> businesses and although markets have of late not been kind to them, many older generations of Americans have nonetheless utilized the opportunity while the going was good to build up equity and assets. Additionally, many have also formed crucial business contacts and clientele over the years. (A good reputation is priceless…a hell of an advantage to have in times of crisis.) <u>Direct beneficiaries of a credit boom</u>, it might be said that previous generations, given original expectations, share a common experience of having <u>beaten the odds</u> and/or having <u>exceeded expectations</u>. Not so for Y-ers. In contrast, Y-ers (literally ambushed by economic realities on the ground) are faced with the sobering fact of soaring joblessness at a most critical juncture in their lives -- just at the point many are endeavoring to establish themselves in the job market. This, it turns out, is wreaking havoc with their work plans and prospective careers. Furthermore, since many possess only nominal work experience, and have little access to start up capital, Y-ers suffer **disproportionately** in the job market, with unemployment rates reaching nearly double the national average. If all this weren't bad enough…when layoffs are announced, Gen Y-ers often find themselves the first to be let go due to their lack of work experience. When presented with job offers below their expectations, young, wide-eyed, idealistic Y-ers are likely to pass up on the positions, naïvely staking their hopes on much-touted news reports hyping a "V" shaped recovery. In contrast, older generations often end up snagging these very same jobs as they enjoy a practical-mindedness that comes with maturity and age. Thus, Gen Y-ers, wet behind the ears, lacking a comprehensive view of the world or thorough understanding of global economics or geo-politics (to say

WOE TO GENERATION "Y"

nothing as to the gravity of the economic maelstrom facing America and the world) face the real possibility of <u>underachieving.</u>

In stark contrast to Gen. Y-ers, the youngest generation, generation "Z" (also known as the 9/11 generation) are to a large degree insulated from the full impact of our global economic calamity by virtue of fate. Most Z-ers (born year 2000 or later) are squarely in the middle of their formative years -- busy attending school. When the time comes for them to spread their wings and reach for the stars (though I expect the world to be wholly unrecognizable from what it is today in all the wrong ways, post economic devastation), one can envision them entering a job market with the possibility of legitimate "green (economic) shoots" sprouting out and about. It is my hope that by the time the majority of Gen. Z-ers are ready to enter the job marketplace the 21st Century Great Global Depression will have largely played out. Some Z-ers will no doubt be called upon to conspire with their predecessors, Gen Y-ers, to help lead the world (at a minimum, the West) out of what will likely be a most bleak chapter in human history through their clever use of talent, innovation, sophistication, and creativity etc. Fifteen, perhaps twenty years from now as many of our major markets will have bottomed out, new industries and technologies will be rife to explode with new possibilities and potential for growth. Likely, our youngest generations working in concert with one another will help **lead our nation as well as other nations to a new era of prosperity.** (The markets will by this time have had plenty of time to sort out the winners from losers, winning industries from older outdated, obsolete industries, new business models from older/defunct outdated models... the wheat from the chaff.)

So where does this leave Y-ers? For starters, Generation Y has a tall task in beginning their productive work years in the midst of a firestorm of global deflation and deleveraging. Those that are more daring are likely to succeed by striking out on their own using their ingenious internet skills in starting their own businesses, or perhaps in helping to solve many of society's problems through innovation and avant-garde, futuristic, outside the box thinking.

Otherwise, under current circumstances it is best that the majority of Generation Y-ers recognize the importance of hunkering down, staying grounded, tempering their inspiration and flare for idealism and hope for the future, and wrapping themselves squarely in **survival mode**. Rallying around family and friends is a good start; using their skills in helping to meet their family's needs all the while maintaining a flexible work posture, bartering for work, reducing their expectations of salary, lifestyle, travel, vacations, and schooling, all serve to reflect smart, beneficial, and practical behavior. A rapid metamorphosis is needed **now** in the thinking pattern and behavior of Gen Y-ers if they are to successfully adapt to the current ongoing economic maelstrom and our vastly and rapidly changing world of credit contraction, deleveraging, falling global commerce, and rising unemployment.

20

BOND MARKET BLOW-UP
CHINA, JAPAN, INDIA, BRAZIL ET AL. (CREDITOR NATIONS OF THE WORLD) HOLD THE KEYS TO AMERICA'S FUTURE, PLUS INTEREST RATES AND WHY THEY <u>MUST</u> CONTINUE TO CLIMB

If you were looking for a Jim Rogers "<u>end of the world as we know it</u>" scenario, this would likely qualify. Based on the <u>ever-falling quality of our debt</u> (US treasuries), and due to a continuous deterioration of Uncle Sam's fiscal standing (ever-growing balance sheet of insurmountable debt), it would not be surprising to wake up one day in the future to witness a **mass liquidation of US bonds** taking place -- one of a multitude of likely triggers being a downgrade of US debt by one or more of our ratings agencies: Fitch, Standard & Poor's, or Moody's. Mind you, most current **trends** point to an eventual weakening of the US bond market: 1) Nation states from around the world have substantially slowed new purchases of US treasury debt, turning off the lending spigots as plans and preparations are presently being drawn up by some for an eventual substitution of the US dollar as world reserve currency. 2) The US budget deficit continues to soar, putting pressure on interest rates. 3) Creditor nations are toughening their stance as they increasingly balk at the prospect of going along on a <u>wild inflationary ride into the abyss</u>, as current US government policies spur on the potential for downgrades in the value of US debt and a further devaluation of US currency. 4) The specter of global sovereign debt (bond) market defaults is on the rise. (Just in the past few months the price to insure several European bond markets has risen sharply, indicating a growing possibility/likelihood of bond market defaults.) 5) The US bond market is severely overbought from a technical as well as a fundamental perspective.

One factor in our favor: Due to the fact that a large portion of US bonds are held by/concentrated in the hands of a handful of foreign governments, the US enjoys a natural <u>hedge</u> as these major bondholders (China alone owns nearly 2 trillion dollars' worth of US treasuries) are discouraged from mass selling, as it is likely to lead to a sharp drop in the bond market (<u>selling</u> of bonds causes **rates to rise** just as conversely, the <u>buying</u> of bonds causes a <u>strengthening</u> of the bond market and **yields to fall).** That said, the primary trend remains intact; creditors' appetite for ever riskier bonds is expected to continue to fall, and selling pressure is thereby projected to <u>build</u>.

Why worry? If just <u>one</u> major bond holder/nation holding a large quantity of US debt were to commence cashing out a large quantity of US debt -- and selling momentum grew (selling often begets more selling) -- a mass liquidation, widespread panic, stampede for the exits, or rout in the markets would not be out of the realm of possibility. (No one wants to be the last one left holding the bag.) Insofar as today is concerned, we continue to keep our creditors at bay…the question is for how long?

Who's in charge?

Creditor nations hold the <u>keys</u> to debtor nations' economies and futures (think of creditor nations as good ol' "debt servicers"). Typically, they are in the business of collecting *principal* and *interest* payments on moneys borrowed. Everything begins and ends with them: <u>they</u> are the **big enchilada** as <u>they</u> control the purse strings; <u>they</u> prop up our economy (or not); <u>they</u> hold the power to extend credit on a whim or deny credit for any one of a multitude of reasons or for no reasons given whatsoever. <u>They have the leverage to</u>

say "jump" and we have the responsibility to respond "how high? Universal laws of lending hold that repayment of borrowed capital is not comprised merely of making interest-only payments (as we are currently doing). **All debts will eventually need to be reconciled!**

Pardon the list of clichés, but…one can only run from his/her creditors for so long…borrowing from Peter to pay Paul must eventually come to a stop…a day of reckoning will arrive sooner or later…the piper must be paid! Just as in instances when a person is successful in temporarily thwarting his creditors or evading his/her debt collectors, or when a person lives on "borrowed" time (please excuse the pun), using one credit card to pay another -- there comes a **point of no return**. At some point (often at the point of insolvency) borrowing becomes so expensive that even paying interest alone becomes too burdensome.

Creditor nations enjoy the upper hand in relation to debtor nations in other ways as well: Today's creditor nations (with the exception of China and her super-heated, overleveraged banking and real estate sectors) have exhibited a good deal more fiscal restraint and fiscal discipline (less money printing and spending) through the current economic crisis than their counterparts in the West -- the world's largest economies -- the US and Eurozone. Creditor nations have not taken to inflating on the same scale as has Uncle Sam through a parade of stimulus packages, massive money printing, bailouts, and currency injections. (As such, one would be hard pressed to find a currency anywhere in the world in more danger of rapid devaluation and hyperinflation as the US greenback -- Jim Rogers refers to it as a "terribly flawed currency.") Countries displaying even a semblance of fiscal restraint while displaying the courage in making painful adjustments to their economies -- defending their currencies and/or refraining from excessive spending and money printing -- will invariably and ultimately be rewarded for restraint shown. As the world emerges from the 21st Century Great Global Depression, **they** will be the ones on a fast track to prosperity.

Why higher interest rates?

Until recently, most of America's global partners were fully committed to keeping the global liquidity party going. However, creditor nations today have begun to take stock of lessons learned from the recent US-led economic collapse. They are recognizing the deteriorating fundamentals of the US bond market and many are increasingly indicating the need to reduce exposure to US treasury debt, some apparently fearing that the worst is yet to come and that the stage is being set for a "get what you can while you still can" scenario. (As such, Americans' **"fix"** increasingly can no longer be relied upon.) Even without a widespread selloff of bonds, the market has presently begun to show signs of stress, with rates for insuring debt on the rise as a consequence of higher risk being built into the system. Also directly affecting interest rates has been the unprecedented buying up of US treasury bonds by the US Treasury and Federal Reserve (QE1 and QE2/Quantitative Easing 1 & 2). As this policy is intended only as a temporary measure, once buybacks slow or stop, interest rates on US bonds will begin to climb precipitously.

America is in a pickle: With foreigners putting the brakes on new debt purchases and the US Treasury and Fed pledging (sometime in the future) to refrain from further bond market purchases, a natural consequence is higher rates. Some may argue that higher interest rates are exactly what's needed -- a critical component in rebalancing our economy, in promoting further sustainable economic expansion, fighting inflation, and increasing fiscal economic health and equilibrium. No matter, for now we can only observe as hope for America in all her manifest destiny to maintain her **independence** and **control of her own destiny** slips away.

A caveat for today's oil-rich nations...

Countries with a monopoly on today's oil market hold the coveted

BOND MARKET BLOW-UP

position of being able to objectively <u>rule the earth</u> in an era of high inflation or hyperinflation. Possessing the keys to the global economy, the world -- already beholden to these nations -- would in the advent of high inflation become even more dependent, ultimately <u>totally reliant</u> on oil-exporting nations. (Incidentally, one can see how the stage is being set for mass conflicts over **black gold**...skirmishes, regional conflicts, and even major wars between nations.) Though I personally expect oil to trade lower before ultimately spiking, the secular bull story for oil (as well as commodities) remains intact: falling world reserves juxtaposed with a secular growing demand for oil by developing nations is likely to spur on <u>strong profits</u>.

It's the long haul that spells trouble for today's economically un-diverse, <u>single industry (oil) nation states</u> as they are likely to suffer a <u>catastrophic fall</u>. For now, leverage remains with oil-rich nations as each successive day brings the world one day closer to the exhaustion of natural resources. On the other hand, once a new "green" economy takes root -- be it 20, 25, or even 50 years from now, G.D.P. as well as net revenues for oil-rich nations are likely to drop like a stone. As such, it is fair to say that each successive day brings oil-rich nation states **one day closer to the end of their respective eras of prosperity**. In so saying, nations that hold the keys to the global economy today -- Saudi Arabia, Iran, Russia, Iraq, Venezuela, etc. are faced with the challenge of diversifying their economies while the going is good or suffer dire consequences, ending up on the dole of the world.

21

GLOBAL DEFLATION AND DELEVERAGING PLAY OUT
"BEARS" ROAM THE EARTH UNOPPOSED

For good reason, the "doom and gloom" crowd (present company included) believes that our current economic problems are likely, in the end, to trump those of the Great Depression

Today, America's fiscal status (as compared to yesteryear) is far more fragile, thereby leaving Americans in a far weaker position to weather the onslaught of severe economic headwinds. **For one**, America's manufacturing base has been hollowed out and cannot be relied upon as a force of economic strength and stability as it has in the past. Can you hear the giant sucking sound (a reference used by former presidential candidate Ross Perot in 1992 to describe the impact of NAFTA, the North American Free Trade Agreement; an agreement which he believed would result in the loss of many US jobs across the border to Mexico)? Not even Ross Perot could have imagined (just two decades later) how many US jobs would actually be lost to Asia, the Pacific Rim, Eastern Europe, the Middle East, and other developing countries. **Second**, America no longer holds the title of world's largest creditor nation; rather, we have assimilated so far as to become the world's largest debtor nation. **Third,** excesses created in our economy today by virtue of our recent boom are substantially larger than those created in the late 1920s. **Fourth,** US consumers are today far more indebted than ever before (as high as ten times more as compared to the average American during the late 1920s). **Fifth,** due to the fact that the world's economies are far more intertwined today as compared with the past, a collapse of US credit markets and consumer spending is reverberating throughout all corners of the globe; America accounts for a full 25% of world commerce, and thus America's collapse by its very nature translates to a global economic collapse. Exacerbating our problems, most major economies of the world are currently experiencing their own versions of an economic tsunami -- collapsing real estate prices, credit contraction, increased joblessness, etc. All of these factors and many more in combination with one another lead me to assert that the fallout from the 21st Century Great Global Depression is likely to exceed the Great Depression.

Summing up future events:

Regarding the Great Global Depression...<u>it too shall come to pass</u>; however, the G.G.D. is not likely to end until certain markers are met: Before all is said and done, look for a wholesale falling out-of-favor for stock/bond/mutual fund (equity) investing (a world away from current market sentiment), continued machinations and implosions in the insolvent, toxic debt-laden global banking system with a likelihood of thousands of more US bank failures (during the Great Depression 9,000 banks went out of business), a further freezing up and dislocation of credit markets, possibly at a level worse than those seen at the height of our current banking crisis -- in late 2008, a collapse in the US commercial real estate market as well as further price deflation in the global residential real estate markets (expect a correction of over 50%+ peak to trough), a contraction of global equity markets to the tune of between 75%-90% (peak to trough), further deleveraging of the derivatives markets, a massive escalation in personal and retail bankruptcies, and so on. Conditions preceding this economic slump were not created overnight. Many decades of excesses will need to be trimmed from the global economy and worked out of the system before a meaningful recovery can take place.

Potential for more economic carnage...

Once the deflationary and deleveraging phase is complete, more chapters from the 21st Century Great Global Depression will still need to be written: Look for a prospective bond market collapse/ mass exodus out of the US treasury market, a sharp falloff in the value of the US dollar and by extension a sizeable loss in buying power for US dollar holders, a strong likelihood of a flare-up of inflation or the emergence of hyperinflation, price escalation across the entire spectrum of products sold, as well as oil, commodities, gold, natural gas prices, etc. going through the roof. All told, in the end, there is a likelihood that conditions will become so unpalatable that we may find ourselves looking back nostalgically at the good ol' days when all we had to deal with was a severe credit deflation, high unemployment, and a large-scale real estate crisis. By my account, we're only now entering the 2nd or 3rd inning of the G.G.D. (Great Global Depression).

22

ENTER, HYPERINFLATIONARY TSUNAMI
LIVING IN THE TWILIGHT YEARS OF THE US DOLLAR

The few benefits that deflation bringeth in terms of lower prices and affordability, inflation taketh away; nowhere to run, no place to hide…

Can you conceive of a world torn apart with a virtual lack of sanctuary, safe houses, and/or safety nets for holding and protecting one's (paper assets) moneys? Can you bring yourself to imagine a nightmare scenario -- even in the most remote realm of possibilities -- that entire personal fortunes, corporations, whole nations could be bankrupted, wiped out in a matter of days? Can you envision a world where even stashing money away under 24/7 armed guard or placing it in an indestructible vault is still a fool's game? Should hyperinflation rear its ugly head and grace our economy with its presence, prices on all goods would instantaneously skyrocket, with many goods and services becoming instantly unavailable and unaffordable; the much-talked-about greatest transfer of wealth in human history (from West to East) would finally commence in earnest:

Some, including the Grand Poobah of forecasting Jim Rogers, now predict the emergence of an "inflationary holocaust" which he describes as a likely consequence from excessive money printing by US and global treasuries and the gross dumping of said moneys into the global economy. Why a "holocaust"? Ramifications of a gross devaluation in global currencies (especially the US dollar) hit so close to home for so many because of the US dollar's position in the world as world reserve currency and the relationship of **cause and effect.** Fallout from a US dollar inflation would affect a virtual *Who's Who* of global US dollar currency holders -- every single American as well as most foreign investors, holders of US debt, world governments, world banks, etc. (Deflation, by contrast, predominantly negatively affects smaller numbers -- holders of tangible assets: real estate, equities, cars, furniture, collectibles, personal possessions, land, technology, and private enterprises.)

Use it or lose it...

Faced with a hyper-inflating dollar, good citizens from all corners of the globe (especially Americans) would face a **trial by fire** (you think Black Friday shopping is stressful?) in terms of trying to spend their evermore worthless dollars on consumer staples or anything else they could find in the wake of a collapsing currency. Vibrations would be felt immediately in the emergence of oil shocks (spikes), skyrocketing prices of household items including food and commodities, as well as a bond market collapse (one of the last remaining mega-bubbles on earth) with soaring interest rates to follow. US federal, state, and local governments would absorb a major brunt of the collapse, with the Fed printing quadrillions of dollars just to keep critical programs active. Consumer confidence and consumer spending would fall to zero, precipitating a further implosion of America's economy with entire sectors and segments of Americans going broke. Americans would grow vastly poorer in relation to other nations, especially to those with fundamentally sound currencies.

Can you get your mind around $40,000 for a gallon of gas? How does $30,000 sound for a bagel? Or how about spending $75 billion dollars to purchase your first (starter) home??? All this and much more is possible in the wonderful world of the magical inflationist Ben Bernanke. Blessed with the ability to create streams of money out of thin air or create an illusion of an economy in recovery, he also has the **power to make debts disappear.** (One caveat, though…his magic tricks and illusions have the unfortunate effect of simultaneously vaporizing the economy, our currency, as well as our way of life for more than a generation.) Think the oil spike of 2008 was bad? You ain't seen nothing yet! In the advent of hyperinflation, with oil prices launching to the moon, heating and cooling homes would instantly become a luxury. Go for a drive? Not happening either. A run on the dollar is likely to create food shortages, especially in consumer staples, with civil and social unrest to follow (really, this goes without saying). Flight to quality and away from the evermore worthless dollar would lead to panic in the streets from New York to Tokyo, from Sydney to Zaire, London to Rio.

No one can predict the exact time or pace at which the dollar is likely to begin its final plunge into oblivion. We can only speculate as to whether the dollar will steadfastly decline at say, a mere 15%-20% per year, or whether the fall will take the shape of a 50% loss of value month over month, or whether a massive crash will occur over a multi-day or multi-week period, ending the dollar's nearly 100-year reign atop the currency food chain. In the end, neither the pace at which the dollar crashes nor whether the dollar ends up hyper-inflating to thousands or trillions of percent will matter all that much. A simple 90%-95% fall would suffice to render the dollar largely worthless and irrevocably change the way we live forever (a far lesser devaluation would do the trick, for that matter).

What we know with a fair degree of certainty is that over time **all fiat currencies fail**. (The US dollar became a fiat currency since it was de-pegged from the gold standard in 1973.) Add to this the fact that we are currently witnessing the largest, most coordinated (global) effort to inflate since the advent of humankind, and we arrive at a place with **parameters and variables, precise consequences, and outcomes that no one can predict with certainty…only speculate about.** Will our hyperinflation scenario play out à la 1920s Weimar

Germany, with US greenbacks (and euros) ending up being used as toilet paper? Perhaps. Suffice it to say once the game's afoot…in the little time it would take for us to debate some of the possible ramifications of hyperinflation, damage would already be palpable.

Hyperinflation and its nasty implications; how it disproportionately affects the middle class:

Some will argue that the <u>rich,</u> owning a majority stake of America's wealth, will have the most to lose from an economic calamity such as this, while others will adamantly claim it is the <u>poor</u> living day to day, on the edge, that will be in the worst position to weather extreme economic conditions. Yet most experts believe it is the <u>middle class</u> that is likely to take the brunt of the wallop from <u>hyperinflation.</u> The vast bulk of citizens living on Main Street are **dangerously positioned** -- having just the right mix of assets/personal possessions, liabilities (debts), and an employment picture to boot that could cause them to <u>lose everything</u> in the event of hyperinflation. Already, Americans' ability to hold onto their middle-class lifestyles typically hinges on <u>maintaining current levels of employment</u> (an increasingly difficult task). In fact, many American households, due to a complete lack of savings and emergency funds, are often <u>one job loss away from total economic devastation</u> (the difference in being able to retain their home, car(s), and maintain their current status in the world). Faring better, the rich often enjoy the diversification that comes with having their wealth spread out over a number of asset classes and/or financial instruments and typically benefit from a healthy income to boot. By contrast, the poor, ironically, at present benefit from the many established public safety nets -- a combination of government assistance and aid from public/private charities which provide a measure of safety in helping to weather a perfect economic storm.

A shell game?

ENTER, HYPERINFLATIONARY TSUNAMI ➤

Finally, relying on Uncle Sam for one's <u>retirement benefits</u> (currently our federal government owes more than 70 trillion dollars in "unfunded liabilities" to entitlement programs) is much like counting on Bernie Madoff to run your 401K plan. With our current social services' trust funds bleeding into the red far faster than previously expected due to a severe fallout in federal tax revenue, the US government is fast running out of money to maintain the size of current and future payouts. Incidentally, all was hunky dory in <u>Bernie Madoff land</u> while the going was good and he was able to maintain capital gains payouts to clients; the racket went belly up and **all hell broke loose** when his ability to maintain dividend/capital gains payouts to clients dried up.

The quick fix for our entitlement programs? Perhaps now would be a good time for government to consider creating *yet a new asset bubble* (as it's done so many times in the recent past -- see Chapter Two and Alan Greenspan's stewardship over the Age of Bubbles) to help mitigate the effects from the fallout/collapse of our insolvent Social Security, Medicare, and Medicaid programs. Regardless, it would be wise for most Americans not to become too complacent in relying on future federal government payouts (social services, retirement benefits, etc.) as their <u>principal</u> or <u>only source of income, retirement or health care benefits</u>, unless and until progress can be made to severely strengthen the underlying and rapidly deteriorating nature of our social services' fiscal balance sheets.

23

BEST CASE SCENARIO
PREPARE YE FOR A PROTRACTED PERIOD OF STAGFLATION

The pitiful, the bad, and the ugly...

Stagflation is a friend to no one, as it typically denotes a bleak phase in the overall economic cycle, embodying the worst possible combination of <u>high inflation</u> and <u>low or stagnant growth</u>. Stagflation is a peculiar economic condition -- an anomaly really, since it is commonplace for inflation to fall during times of economic stagnation. (In most instances, high inflation and falling growth are mutually exclusive.) Nonetheless, when it occurs, stagflation is known for a time of high unemployment, loss of consumer confidence, dollar weakness (often resulting in a drastic drop in purchasing power), skyrocketing prices for wholesale goods, and soaring oil, gold, and commodities markets.

With the majority of economic weather barometers steadily deteriorating and with a perfect storm of economic headwinds heading our way, we should be so lucky to escape with a decade-and-a-half long period of malaise. Otherwise, it is far more likely that our economy will suffer a series of intense, acute, and/or catastrophic insults, purges, and crashes along the way, helping exacerbate, intensify, and accelerate the deterioration and destabilization of the economy. For now all we can do is speculate, but most market watchers, business community leaders, and economists today agree: **a period of higher inflation lies ahead** (be it stagflation, high inflation or hyperinflation). Let us hope it is not the last.

24

ANALOGY TO ARMAGEDDON
2/3 OF WORLD COMMERCE IS WIPED OUT!

Global unemployment reaches biblical proportions as 1/3 of all jobs perish from the earth…

Can you imagine a day in which you wake up to find the unemployed in the US totaling 35-40 or more million or witness our economically hardest-hit states suffering from ("U6") unemployment rates approaching 50%? Can you conceive of a world where many of your friends, neighbors, and relatives have lost their jobs, their homes, or both and are now on the dole of the government or state? Can you envision a world so impoverished and desperate that conflicts are erupting simultaneously all over the globe? **This potential <u>doomsday scenario</u> hinges on whether our current economic calamity/crisis meanders about as a recession (a category 1 or 2 economic storm), or whether it spirals into a full-blown <u>depression</u> (a category 5 "killer" with the power to obliterate and annihilate everything in its path). As a rule, recessions typically last 42 months or so; depressions on the other hand, can often play out over the course of a generation -- averaging 26 years or more. Whether in the end we see our circumstance through the scope of the "R" word (recession) or the "D" word (depression) will impact and shape our lives for the rest of our days.**

◀ 112

ANALOGY TO ARMAGEDDON ➤

The big "D" and how we (prospectively) get there...the numbers do in fact add up:

Let's use the final quarter of 2008 as a guide for an (admittedly) worst-case scenario in calculating job losses; our economy then contracted at an annual pace of 6.3%. Just a few months at this rate of decline (late 2008-early 2009 qualifies) and we are well on our way to achieving jobless numbers in line with the Great Depression.

Here's how: For starters, "healthy" unemployment alone (typically a 4%-5% jobless rate) equates to 1/5th of total joblessness from the Great Depression. (The Great Depression experienced a jobless rate of between 24%-25% at the high.) Add in our recent jobs "meltdown" (an implosion which has brought our current national non-farm jobless rate to roughly 10%) and we arrive at a sum of 2/5 (40%) of the total carnage experienced during the Great Depression. Now instead of using our official government jobless figures, we calculate unemployment using "U6" unemployment (U6 is considered the most comprehensive measure of unemployment as it calculates discouraged workers, "marginally attached" workers, and part-time workers) and we reach a sum of between 17%-18% unemployment (our current actual jobless rate), and nearly ¾ of all joblessness experienced at the height of the Great Depression! [**The official figure used to calculate unemployment during the Great Depression, all the way through and including the recession in the early 1990s was calculated in U6.**] In so saying, when Americans today feel a sense of dread regarding job markets, prospects for work and/or job creation, it is well-justified. (Our "official" near 10% unemployment rate is indeed a **misnomer** as U6 joblessness supports the case for an unemployment epidemic.)

With the prospect of a double-dip recession brewing (a recession taking the shape of a "W") a new round of imploding earnings could spur on new rounds of job cuts and catapult the official unemployment rate to upward of 13%-14% or more (and the actual "unofficial" U6 unemployment rate nearly on par with the Great Depression).

◄ 21ST CENTURY GREAT GLOBAL DEPRESSION

Furthermore, if one were to factor in even just a few of the many <u>major threats and principal factors contributing to America's precipitous decline</u> as described in Chapter Four, it is not hard to imagine **an economic fallout of historic proportions**. Finally, imagine calculating the impact from just a simple majority of the threats listed in Chapter Four, and you arrive at a foundation for **<u>economic fallout well in excess to that of the Great Depression!</u>**

How might a 1/3 contraction of global commerce play out? The imploding US economy in real time:

Starting at the top, the **US real estate market** (homebuilding industry, mortgages brokers, mortgage lenders, real estate agents, property managers, home improvement stores, carpenters, plumbers, electricians, roofers, cementers, other skilled labor, laborers, landscape designers, etc.) in aggregate is <u>severely</u> <u>contracting</u> and is weighing heavily on our overall economy. This industry, mind you, has already been contracting steadily over the past few years at well over 1% annual G.D.P. Problem is, all signs point to more shoes dropping before a sustainable bottom in housing is reached (new wave of adjustable rate resets, insipient crash in commercial real estate, mass commercial real estate vacancies, additional bank failures, assimilation of a burgeoning oversupply of homes, and escalating foreclosures). When all is said and done -- the very industry which <u>expanded</u> to the tune of over 50,000 jobs per month (month over month growth) during the height of the real estate mania is now <u>the epicenter of the Great Global Depression</u> as it continues to <u>shed</u> the same amount of jobs or more per month. According to my calculations, it is likely for the total <u>economic fallout from this industry alone</u> to account for an aggregate drop of between 9%-12% US G.D.P. (gross domestic product) once all the excesses have been purged from the system.

Next, our ailing **financial industry** (still largely insolvent even after massive infusions of liquidity by the Fed) continues to shed jobs with projections of more job losses to come. Bank failures this year continue to outpace bank failures from 2009 by a fairly wide margin -- nearly two hundred hundred banks are projected to fail in 2010 with a further acceleration of failures in the years to follow. With falling real estate markets serving to obliterate bank balance sheets and with an escalation of commercial loan refinances slated over the coming 24-30 months, many key analysts have begun warning of a cascading effect: an avalanche of commercial loan defaults resulting in numerous additional bank failures commencing later this year. All the while, the US banking industry continues to suffer from negative public perception as well as from a perceived lack of credibility after the collapse of Wall Street (despite the Fed's ability to manipulate bank balance sheets to currently reflect positive earnings). Additionally, the recent **apocalyptic loss of wealth throughout the world** virtually necessitates a further contraction of the financial industry. This industry which also lies at the dead epicenter of the global economic crisis is likely to (when all is said and done) shed no fewer than 3-5 million jobs (a conservative estimate) and account for an overall 6%-8% decline in G.D.P.

Another major industrial complex and economic behemoth currently in the midst of an historic contraction, and which is likely to weigh on the overall economy, is our **automotive industry**. The massive contraction and consolidation already underway as a result of recent bankruptcy filings by General Motors (former King of Detroit's "big three") and Chrysler are resulting in substantial job losses throughout the automotive manufacturing industry as well as a loss of employment for auto dealers, auto parts and supply stores etc. In addition, the US automotive industry continues to struggle from a collapse in consumer spending and bank lending. (Sales peaked just a few years back when 17 million new cars and light trucks were sold in the US per calendar year; today the new auto market has imploded by over 50% with only 8-9 million new cars and light trucks projected to sell this year (an optimistic estimate). Furthermore, sales are expected to remain flat for some years to come. <u>Overcapacity</u> in the automotive industry alone will force a contraction of millions of jobs once all critical restructuring has been made. As such, count on a loss of an additional 2%-4% G.D.P. **In sum, the damage from these three industries alone is likely to account for a 21%-24% or more contraction of US G.D.P. (roughly half of the 45%-plus total economic contraction experienced during the Great Depression).**

As you might have imagined, the bad news doesn't stop here. <u>This doesn't even begin to address **overall overcapacity** built up during the bubble/boom years</u>. Even some of the most optimistic and "bullish" projections by leading economists today include an acknowledgment that <u>severe contractions likely lie ahead for a broad spectrum of US and global industries</u> (in addition to the aforementioned industries -- retail, travel, manufacturing, shipping, service sector, technology, the discretionary spending sector, and so on). Factoring in the likelihood of further downsizing of these major industries -- at a conservative 2%-3% G.D.P. each (in addition to other smaller sectors not mentioned here), and one arrives at an additional overall contraction of between 15%-20% G.D.P. -- perhaps 25%-30% or higher. Inventories will need to be worked off, storefronts will need to close, overcapacity and oversupply will need to be sloughed off as a more equitable, sustainable, healthy calibration of supply and demand is restored.

Finally, let's not forget the old adage *"as goes the US economy, so goes the global economy."* Today, the US is intrinsically tied together with its global trading partners and so it is <u>inconceivable for the US economy</u> (accounting for a full 25% of gross global domestic product) <u>to contract independent of other major economies of the world.</u> (Mind you, even in a far less interconnected world during the Great Depression, world commerce fell by nearly 65%.) For now… for better, for worse, for richer, for poorer…America leads and the world follows. In the future, however, countries which take steps to detach and/or divorce themselves from America may do so to their economic benefit.

25

VROOM, VROOM… REVVING UP THE NEW ENGINE OF WORLD GROWTH
"BRIC" NATIONS (Brazil, Russia, India, and China) AS WELL AS OTHER DEVELOPING NATIONS EMERGE AS THE SUPERCHARGER OF WORLD GROWTH

The old engine of the world economy has died and lies in a heap of ash; life in the new acceleration lane…

It does seem that so much in life is often dictated by one's ability (or lack thereof) to identify <u>trends</u>. Trends affect our lives every single day in many overt and subliminal ways; trends, in conjunction with the added leverage of "father time," combine to produce powerful results (take for instance, the <u>compounding effect</u> of royalties or dividends in terms of their ability to impact our lives).

Please consider the following analogy: Two runners line up to race each other in a marathon (a 42-plus kilometer run) whereby the first runner thoroughly outpaces his counterpart from the get go. A dozen kilometers into the race the first runner has built up a seemingly insurmountable lead. However his pace has begun to slow. The second runner is gaining momentum and has now begun consistently clocking in faster kilometers. If this trend continues and the second runner is able to sustain his rate of speed, he will likely reach the finish line with time to spare, perhaps even winning the race by a mile (no pun intended).

This analogy serves to aptly describe the relationship between the United States and China today. While China's economy represents but a fraction of America's economy at present, it consistently gains on its counterpart -- whether at breakneck speed or at times at a more subdued pace -- as it **closes the gap in economic output between the two nations.** (While America's mature economy has bounced between slow growth, no growth, and/or negative growth over the past decade, China's economy has remained vibrant over the same time frame, averaging over 8% growth.) In so saying, we are faced with a **tale of two contrasting empires -- <u>one swiftly in ascent and one stagnating.</u>** Should this <u>powerful trend</u> continue, and it appears that it is likely, the **compounding effects over just the next decade and a half are projected to catapult China to the top of the economic food chain.**

Add to this a whole host of peripheral positive trends running concurrently in China's favor: sound fiscal discipline, focus on building up of infrastructure, shifting of investment focus to tangible assets, gold, and commodities and away from suspect paper/fiat currencies (specifically US bonds), a principled approach to living within its means while displaying a solid work ethic, the building up of a vibrant manufacturing base, a healthy national savings rate -- and one begins to recognize that <u>China's emergence as economic superpower is no accident.</u> As such, China continues to ready itself to **economically dominate**. For the host of reasons described above, as well as many others, comparisons are being made between China's current rise to prominence and America's rise to a status of world power in the earlier part of the 20th century.

Similarly, India, Brazil, Singapore, Mexico, Indonesia, Malaysia, Thailand, and South Korea as well as other developing nations have in recent years consistently shown a propensity for competent stewardship of their often rapidly growing economies, during which time their economies have increasingly become a <u>mainstay of</u>

global manufacturing. These countries, and others which continue to maintain their fiscal houses in order while remaining on a path of sustained positive economic growth, are in the process of reaping the rewards as they become more **self-reliant by the day.** As their economies grow stronger they become increasingly less dependent on America's debased currency, America's bond markets, suspect financial products, and/or banking institutions. Positive secular trends -- increased industrialization, increase in internal consumer consumption and rising living standards, healthy export markets, etc. lead us to the following prediction: These nations are the **burgeoning stars on the rise!**

26

THE RED DRAGON SLAYS THE ONCE ALL-MIGHTY EAGLE
CHANGING OF THE GUARD

World order gets flipped on its head as an "Age of Darkness" descends upon the earth...

The final chapters of the Great Global Depression will likely bring about unspeakable turmoil: a thorough collapse of most major (predominantly Western) markets, oil shocks, mass global bankruptcies, a collapse in world commerce, mass unemployment, social and political unrest leading to (in some instances) a destabilization of nation states, mass poverty or poverty on an unprecedented scale, confusion, war, disease, regional conflicts, geo-political shifts in power, substitution of the US dollar as world reserve currency, gross devaluation of numerous major currencies throughout the world, failure of and a possible abolishment of the US Federal Reserve, collapse in social order, skyrocketing crime, tax revolts, a collapse of the middle class replete with its ensuing fight for survival, conflicts and competition over natural resources, a complete falling-out of materialism/consumerism in favor of security concerns, etc.

Due to the scale of debt amassed from decades-long US policies of fiscal mismanagement, the burning question before us becomes

THE RED DRAGON SLAYS THE ONCE ALL-MIGHTY EAGLE

not "if" but "at what point" does America and her allies (many NATO nations possess far larger debt burdens as a percentage of their G.D.P.s than America) cede their global economic and military dominance throughout the world, receding to a more moderated role in global geopolitics?

"It's the economy, stupid"-- or rather...the global economy, stupid.

Historically speaking, major powers have been built on foundations of economic and military dominance and superiority. So it has been and so shall it be now, during, and after the Great Global Depression. To the victor go the spoils! I submit to you that the victor in this case **is** the economy. (Resilience and strength of one's economy means everything.) As goes one's economy, so goes everything else -- geopolitical rankings, military rankings, etc.

As such, those nations who emerge from the G.G.D. the most economically enduring, as well as the most stable and productive -- including a new breed of fast-growing economies in the developing world -- will take their rightful place among geopolitical decision makers, in time spawning some of the world's strongest militaries/military alliances. Fiscally responsible governments (creditor nations) with healthy budgets and balance sheets will (many for the first time) rise to key roles in the New World Order. Eventually, depending on the degree of collapse of the West, they may be inspired to dictate terms of the New World Order. On the flip side, those that did not manage their affairs well will fall precipitously in stature, or fall completely by the wayside, as has always been the case throughout history.

An unfortunate, yet prevalent historic trend portends a connection between times of economic chaos and unrest and a rise of dictators, dictatorships, tyrants, etc. Political and military power vacuums (often a byproduct of periods of economic turmoil) are typically filled by imperialists, political opportunists, the power

hungry, as well as a plethora of egomaniacs, sociopaths, and villains. Often this occurs as a result of a country's incapacitation from its active and/or visceral role in the greater geopolitical universe of yin/yang, taking its eye off the ball in terms of containing threats. (America's preoccupation with her economic troubles during the 1930s -- post 1929 stock market crash -- is seen as a factor in the rise of the Third Reich and the emergence of Hitler.) Although on occasion some political, military, and/or economic power vacuums are filled peacefully and without conflict, more often than not they are filled by **force.**

The world today remains a dangerous place and the stakes have never been higher. China is starving to assert itself not only as a major geo-political player but as the top economy in the world. New tensions have been steadily rising between Russia and the United States (in spite of today's "Re-set Policy"), with Russia moving to reassert control over former Soviet states and satellites. Other imperialistically leaning nations – Iran, North Korea, and Venezuela continue to assert themselves politically, militarily, and economically in their respective regions and appear hell-bent on shaking up the current World Order. As such, a challenge is being waged against America's leadership throughout the world and of a so-called "unipolar world." Should the 21st Century Great Global Depression play out as I believe it is likely to, an **escalation of threats is all but a foregone conclusion.**

Finally, fluctuating currencies are likely to affect the outcome of the G.G.D., especially as it relates to the US dollar. If American-led inflation runs rampant around the globe, it is likely to guide the timing of global power shifts, fiscal and social upheaval, etc. Nothing, mind you, is more likely to accelerate the changing of the guard to a New World Order or accelerate the greatest transfer of wealth in the history of man than the emergence of high inflation and/or hyperinflation.

27

OUR ENEMIES SMELL BLOOD
AMERICA EITHER SHIFTS TO RENEWABLES OR SINKS INTO OBLIVION

The stakes could not be higher…
American energy independence is an absolute matter of national security. America is catastrophically unprepared for a potential wave of high inflation, hyperinflation, and/or oil spike…

Our present circumstances are reminiscent of a scene from the end of the Star Trek movie "Wrath of Khan" where the Enterprise (seemingly to no avail) is desperately trying to extricate itself from a nebula which is about to explode. Captain Kirk asks, "<u>Distance from Reliance</u>?" (Reliance is another starship positioned virtually atop the Enterprise, armed with a so-called "Genesis Device" that is ready to detonate within moments; it carries with it a capability of annihilating everything within its sights.) The Enterprise proceeds at snail's pace due to damage sustained to its warp core and is quickly <u>running out of time.</u> Commander Chekov answers, "<u>4,000 meters</u>." Kirk looks to his son for guidance as if to ask if the Enterprise will be able to avert disaster. His son shakes his head, indicating **"no."**

This scene aptly serves as a metaphor to describe America's current dire predicament in the world, in that just as the Enterprise appears to be responding to imminent danger "too little too late," America continues to sit like a <u>proverbial dead</u>

duck stuck on its addiction to oil in a world hell-bent on "reflation." Just like the Enterprise… barring a miracle (in the movie Spock gives his life to save the ship and his shipmates), we (specifically America and the West) are faced with a similar prospect of not making it out of our sinister circumstances.

Paying for our sins…

We've squandered every major opportunity to renew, reinvigorate, and restore our economy in recent years when opportunities abounded and now are left to meander through our existence, beholden to everyone for survival, ill-prepared to deal with the future. We **knew** full well (far ahead of our current period of economic chaos) that being inextricably reliant on nation states (regimes) not friendly to us and our interests was a **dangerous game.** We knew we had a mandate to do whatever due diligence was necessary to gain at least a semblance of energy independence by converting a portion of our overall economy to alternative and/or indigenous energy sources: natural gas, nuclear power, coal, oil shale, hybrid-electric technology as well as renewable green technology -- wind, solar, fuel cell technology, thermo-nuclear power, hydro-electric energy, etc. We know without a shadow of a doubt that in the not too distant future the world will be forced to shift to "renewables" (it now appears this may happen sooner than later as natural supplies are in the process of exhausting themselves) but we chose to delay, procrastinate, obfuscate -- **not lead** the world in new technologies to **repower** our lives. Finally, we know with absolute certainty that we are susceptible to the emergence of oil shocks (events that will leave our country vulnerable to our enemies), but we have not safeguarded our nation or our nation's economy in the advent of such events. (Oil spikes are dangerous during times of prosperity and absolutely lethal during times of economic weakness and turmoil.) In sum, we know how our nation's **mission statement** must read -- a solemn obligation to (implicitly and explicitly) live in a world with a keen eye and a focus on the future, but we have done nothing at present, <u>nor shown any vision in preserving our empire</u>. Our actions are totally disconnected from the facts on the ground. **<u>We squandered our greatest opportunities during our boom years to make our economy more self-sufficient and now there will be hell to pay</u>!**

In the interim...

"Going Green" was a favorite theme for liberals twenty and thirty years ago; today it is an essential truth for **<u>both sides of the political aisle</u> as it represents a major component in the endurance of America's sovereignty, a vote for our national security and future, and a <u>win</u> for the environment.** That said, costs for converting our economy to a true "green" economy will take many years and many more dollars. As a result, it is best that America's quest for energy independence not simply be relegated entirely to green technologies at present, and rather should include other <u>alternative energy sources which are plentiful</u>: increased reliance on indigenous energies such as natural gas, coal, oil shale, etc., building of new nuclear power plants, the upgrading of our aging electrical grid as well as increasing our dependence on efficient light rail. We know that American **energy independence** is an <u>absolute moral imperative</u> (no matter one's party or ideology), as excessive oil dependence in today's world is a direct **threat to our national security.** Aren't rational people expected to respond to situations of threat with a sense of self-preservation and responsible action? **I wonder.**

Bracing for impact...

While we cannot change the past, we <u>can</u> look to the future. Inflation may very well be coming down the pike, possibly <u>at a level and of a kind never before seen or experienced in the history of our republic</u>. To be associated with the generation that simply stood by

-- passively watching and witnessing our current economic and geo-political developments taking place around us, while not taking all possible measures to **purge ourselves off "black gold" now** -- may yet prove to be <u>the ultimate catalyst</u> in our undoing.

America's reliance and dependence on foreign nations spans well beyond our energy needs...

With the possible exception of North Korea, we are <u>**absolutely dependent on a chorus of nations which read like a *Who's Who* of the so-called "axis of evil," and/or nations posing the greatest economic challenge or physical threat to America.**</u> For starters, America is totally reliant on China (an economic rival and potential future adversary) as we have grown <u>addicted</u> to routine cash injections via China's longstanding record of US treasury purchases. We are further dependent on a slew of emerging market nations (including China) for low cost products and services as our indigenous manufacturing base continues its plunge to <u>obsolescence</u>. Our largest suppliers of oil -- a number of oil rich OPEC nations (Iran and others), as well as Russia and Venezuela -- help keep our economy afloat, yet continue to espouse imperial ambitions displaying intermittent provocations as well as challenges to Uncle Sam's <u>reign as lone global superpower</u>. **<u>We need energy independence and we need it yesterday</u>; we need to cut our fiscal and economic over-reliance on other nation states even sooner.** Anyone still not convinced that we are <u>not</u> on the right track for the future, then <u>I have a time share in Florida I want to sell you</u>.

28

REBUILDING AMERICA'S MANUFACTURING BASE

AMERICA'S FUTURE HAS THE FOLLOWING SLOGAN/ LABEL ATTACHED TO IT:
"MADE IN AMERICA"

While growing corporate profits is by and large a good thing and an essential part of business, it does have its limitations...

No nation can endure without an indigenous and vibrant manufacturing base, period. In the future, if America is to remain sovereign, relevant, as well as competitive and the American empire is to endure, it must secure a viable, stable, productive, and lasting manufacturing industry. Americans' preoccupation with binge buying, addiction to inexpensive goods, selling their souls (and posterity) for instant gratification will need to stop. Separating the difference between recognizing the importance of global trade, and relying on cheap goods and products to the point that it leads to permanent job losses (detracting from our economic health) is essential. Displaying restraint, maturity, and vigilance as it relates to our economic concerns -- striking a balance between free trade while maintaining a vibrant home-grown manufacturing base -- is the duty of all sovereign nations.

Citizens must be made to realize that buying products **made in America** not only helps alleviate the gross imbalances in our trade deficits, stimulating growth in our gross domestic product, but that it acts as a natural prophylactic against job loss, buffering our economy in times of economic turmoil. Companies will have to do their part as well (as in the case of our ailing automotive industry) and work to regain customer loyalty by producing higher-quality products at more competitive prices. More importantly however, US companies will need to recognize the need to <u>mitigate and balance their desire for profit with the necessity of maintaining a vibrant presence of US workers</u>. Abject ferrying off of jobs overseas must be recognized as a short-sighted policy which is likely to directly and indirectly harm profits down the road. Government will need to act <u>aggressively</u> and <u>proactively</u> to impose fair trade policies with other nations.

From time to time we all enjoy the perks of buying low cost products manufactured in countries where lower wage structures prevail: China, India, Pakistan, Thailand, Indonesia, Mexico, Turkey, Eastern Europe et al. Speaking for myself, I can report feeling giddy following the purchase of an item which I am able to procure at say 30-40 cents on the dollar. It does have the effect of leaving an impression of building <u>instant wealth</u>. However when I carefully weigh the various consequences (for our nation, for our macro-economy and for our future) for that moment of joy, or that rush of excitement I experienced, the feeling of nirvana quickly dissipates.

So dependent are we on imports today that if push came to shove and for one reason or another global trade was disrupted (specifically our access to imported goods) mass chaos would ensue. Quickly our store shelves would go bare as we would begin to instantaneously run out of a majority of products sold "stat" (including common, often essential everyday products): food, furniture, apparel, toys, cosmetic items, household products, diapers, utensils, kitchenware, pots and pans, toilet paper, technology, stationery products, sporting equipment, computers, video games, etc. *Imagine the fallout* *if (God forbid) we entered an extended trading war with China, India, or Mexico? How would we continue to handle our affairs and all the while prevent the <u>sky from falling</u>? What would happen in the instance where we were all suddenly forced to obtain the vast majority of our food products from a dwindling group of local or domestic vendors, or go to the black market (actively <u>compete</u> with others) to purchase basic consumer staples at substantially marked up prices?*

Let me guess…the concept of buying products <u>made in America</u> doesn't sound so passé or "hokey" anymore, now does it? **In fact it symbolizes patriotism, it is a vote for sovereignty, it is a vote of confidence…of economic reason and responsible citizenship and a vote for an adherence to our cumulative futures.**

BACK TO BASICS -- self-sacrifice and working for a better tomorrow:

To preserve our way of life, we will (as a nation) need to adapt the very essence in how we think and act, at first using baby steps to deprogram our national mindset of recent years. It will necessitate <u>living within our means, refraining from purchases we cannot afford, and restoring fiscal sanity</u> to America (federal, state, local governments, citizens, and corporations). Thus we will **renew America** and restore our standing in the world. Such is life in the grand cycles of boom and bust.

29

DARE TO DREAM: REACHING FOR THE PINNACLE YET AGAIN ONE SMALL STEP AT A TIME
AMERICA'S RETURN FROM THE ASHES BEGINS WITH THE BELIEF THAT BETTER DAYS LIE AHEAD

At some point the only direction left to go is up...

A severely humbled nation, America emerges less influential, no longer the purveyor of world reserve currency, no longer the word's sole superpower (perhaps not a superpower at all). America is forced to go back to her roots of sane fiscal stewardship as she emerges leaner, smarter, wiser, more mature, and a more fiscally responsible nation among nations. (What a high price to pay for the reckless mismanagement of our affairs!)

A silver lining?

Despite the specter of a coming plethora of economic, geo-political, social, and security concerns and woes: falling markets, a crashing currency, social upheaval, bankrupting of our entitlement programs, harsh macro-economic realities, soaring joblessness and homelessness, skyrocketing crime, food shortages, runs on banks, loss of US prestige and influence in the world, loss of economic and military might, global instability, and chaos…<u>**AMERICA WILL NOT CEASE TO EXIST!**</u>

After twenty-eight chapters of abundantly gloomy forecasts, I am pleased to present the flip side of the coin, the light at the end of the tunnel: For even in the advent of a worst case scenario in which 2/3 of worldwide commerce (G.D.P.) is shed, America would still possess a <u>five trillion dollar economy (in today's dollar terms), still good enough to "**place**"</u> using the old racing metaphor of **<u>win-place-show.</u>** <u>(Retaining the coveted 2nd place in the global economy is still impressive by any standard.)</u>

The circle of life…(from rags to riches)

For Americans, the end of the 21st Century Great Global Depression will arrive not a moment too soon after a long, drawn-out period of economic pain, turmoil, and chaos -- <u>but arrive it shall</u>. Life in America as well as in the rest of the world around us will be dramatically altered but Americans (if history is any guide) are a resilient bunch and will not allow ourselves to be swept into oblivion either. Once the great secular bear market has ended with the dead last bull throwing in the towel, Americans -- <u>offspring of the old "pioneer" spirit, a headstrong people with a take-no-prisoners mentality</u> -- will come back with a vengeance! We have endured great struggles in our past and will do so again with dignity and honor so long as we stand united. As we will be forced to **think anew** and **reshape the very essence of capitalism**, <u>we will fare better for it in the end</u>. Once the transformation is complete, a new era of prosperity will unfold from the deepest, darkest shadows. The "new" America will approach fiscal and budgetary matters with sophistication, reconciling our budgets as we go while rejecting the notion of unlimited borrowing as a means to a better life. Our housing market declines will have ended, foreclosures will have dried up as excess inventory will finally have been cleared out. As to

America's preoccupation with possessions and tangible assets -- it will cease after a long, drawn-out period of time and eventually begin to emerge again -- alongside, remarkably, a new thirst for paper assets (life's a circle). At some point, job losses will slow, stop, and begin to turn around for good. Our image and standing in the world post-enduring a severe pummeling will rise again; <u>do not discount the abundance of goodwill that exists in the world toward America and Americans</u> in general.

Nothing but the best will do…(leading by example)

Shedding the notion that we are the chosen ones, somehow or other destined to be the greatest superpower for all time is critical. As I've reiterated numerous times, remaining the beacon of hope throughout the world will require us to walk the walk and talk the talk, to lead by example. To restore the admiration, respect, and adoration of others will require America to <u>showcase her unique and abundant talents and blessings for all the world to see</u> -- never embracing our shortcomings or meandering as a nation of underachievers. We'll need to outperform, out-compete, out-excel other nations in <u>key</u> <u>areas</u> such as education, healthcare, technology, renewable "green" innovation, banking, investment, farming, even manufacturing. Leading the world to a new chapter of humankind identified by an era of unimaginable technological advancement and a new **green** global economy could very likely be the <u>key</u> that unleashes America's entrepreneurial spirit, <u>bringing her back to the pinnacle of world power and success.</u> Just as World War II is credited for bringing America out of the Depression, so too might new developments in green technology serve as catalysts to a dawning of a new era of economic prosperity.

Forced cutbacks…

Controlling spending (government, corporate, and personal)

means a thorough review of all budgets, <u>cutting unnecessary waste</u> wherever possible: military budgets will need to be adjusted if it is proven that they are helping to bankrupt America; cuts in entitlement programs must be made if the programs continue to run in the red; regulating and reforming critical aspects of the financial industry/letting the free markets decide the fate of failed companies, industries, and institutions is key. Having citizens refrain from excessive speculation, downgrading our lifestyles to regain fiscal balance, increasing our focus on civility and philanthropy -- helping out one another especially in times of trouble -- are all <u>necessary ingredients</u> in allowing us to get back in the saddle. Bartering for goods, increasing volunteerism and/or donations to charities…each of us will be called upon to do our part to build a sustainable, prosperous America.

In closing…

Alas, although things are likely to get much worse before they get better, there will come a day when Americans will once again begin to look at the future with a renewed sense of optimism, believing that <u>America's best days are ahead</u> while recognizing the proverbial "pinnacle" is once again <u>before us</u> (never behind). <u>It is at this seminal point that America's turnaround will begin in earnest.</u>

Then, striving on with the <u>same determination and sacrifice that characterized our ancestors</u> to build a better tomorrow, we must pledge never again to lose sight of our core ideals and values; we must consistently raise expectations in ourselves, meet our challenges with unwavering courage, etc. Appealing to our better natures with newfound inspiration (just as we have so many times in the past), we must proceed to restore the image of America as a shining city on the hill -- only this time we must <u>pledge to build it ground up with **indestructible** beams of steel (with depleted uranium for added strength), coated with diamonds and pearls, sporting streets of</u>

platinum. A new breed of leaders with bold new visions will emerge and be called to inspire America to yet a new era of promise. May God bless us and restore all of us; may our nation heal itself and find common purpose, and may God guide us on **bold winds of change** as we endeavor to **renew** our **great union**. God Bless.

FAVORITE QUOTES and EXPRESSIONS

Jim Rogers: (quote from an interview in 2004 regarding future prospects for the US and global economy) He predicted, "It's the end of the world as we know it."

Peter Schiff: Speaking to the fundamentals of our current US economy vs. America's economy of the past, he drew this contrast: "America manufactured its way into prosperity and consumed its way into bankruptcy."

Jim Rogers: "Sometimes I wonder if our central bank is just going to print money until we run out of trees."

Samuel Taylor Coleridge: "And in today already walks tomorrow." (Quotation used as mantra by economic and political prognosticator Gerald Celente)

Michael Panzner: Drawing a parallel between ancient Rome and modern day America (I paraphrase): During the end times of the Roman Empire when it was in decay -- social, political, moral, economic etc. -- the public was fed bread and circuses in an effort to keep it satiated. Today's equivalent: Nascar, reality TV and video gaming.

Warren Buffett: "It's only when the tide goes out that you learn who's been swimming naked."

Jim Rogers: Speaking in regard to the dilemma of America's burgeoning indebtedness and lack of capital reserves, he stated: "In America, you don't have reserves…you either have to **tax** it, **print** it, or **borrow** it -- none of which is good for anybody."

Rick Ackerman: In an article titled "Chasing stocks while Rome burns" published in February 2008, Mr. Ackerman questioned investor wisdom in maintaining a superfluously positive posture toward stocks in light of crumbling fundamentals in the US and global economy.

Warren Buffet: "I'd be a bum on the street with a tin cup if the markets were always efficient."